snatch

THE SCREENPLAY

GUY RITCHIE

snatch
THE SCREENPLAY

GUY RITCHIE

ORION

First published in 2000 by Orion Media
An imprint of Orion Books Ltd
Orion House, 5 Upper St Martin's Lane
London WC2H 9EA

A CIP catalogue record for this book is available from
the British Library.

ISBN 0-75283-772-9

Text design and layout by Essential Books

Printed and bound in Great Britain by
Clays Ltd, St Ives Plc.

CONTENTS

INTRODUCTION

I have worked on two films now; the first was contaminated by anxiety due to several factors. For example, whether the money would be there for the next day's shooting, did I know what I was doing – or did anybody else, come to that? I tried not to let these insecurities trouble me, and I did my best not to let them show, so I bobbed along laughing, joking and slapping people on their backs whenever I saw the slightest window of opportunity; in reality my arse was clapping like a drum.

On 'Snatch', however, I was dogged by a different set of problems. It wasn't anything to do with money or confidence this time; it was due to a synchronous conspiracy from cast and crew. On this film I had every desire and intention of being seen and taken as a more developed and more serious director.

But apparently it didn't matter what I thought, because everybody fuckin' ignored my new-found sincerity and seriousness. My reputation from the last film for back-slapping and laughing at inane jokes was now haunting me,

so from the word go everybody thought they'd have a jolly up. The cast and crew thought my new-found stern looks and conversations were sarcastic efforts at taking the piss. So in turn they thought they would take the piss, and consequently they fucked about from the first day to the last. How we managed to actually get the film in the can is a head-scratching mystery.

That said, they must have done something right because they delivered more than the goods asked for, and they delivered them in record time. It has been an enlightening experience and a strange privilege to have directed both these films, and if this is what arsing about awards you, I only hope to witness more of it in the future.

Guy Ritchie
August 2000

ABOUT THE CAST...

ADE (Tyrone) plays a selfish role. In his film debut as big Tyrone, he prizes his car above all else but he isn't much of a getaway driver for Vinny and Sol, the pawnbroker duo turned robbers. He disagrees constantly with his passengers – and their dog, wishing it harm or death given the chance as it drools over his car seats. Ade (he prefers to go by just the one name) is a mover and a shaker on the London scene representing a number of promising bands and individuals such as The Foot Long Heroes and Sacha Stone.

ANDY BECKWITH (Errol) leaves a formidable imprint of East End clout as Errol, one of Brick Top's henchmen. Beckwith has worked in the building trade for most of his life and manages a very successful Sunday League. He has performed in Willie Russell's 'Stags and Hens' and his first major public appearance was with Wee Lassie Productions at the Groucho Club, London, in 'Last Orders'.

EWEN BREMNER (Mullet) is perfect in this almost cameo role of a hard-nosed grass. Bremner has had a very successful film, TV and theatre career and will be remembered, if not loved, as the sheet-clutching Spud in 'Trainspotting'. Bremner has also appeared in 'Judge Dredd' and as Archie in Mike Leigh's 'Naked'. His theatre credits include two productions of 'Trainspotting' in which he took the part of Renton, and John Byrne's comedy 'The Slab Boys Trilogy' playing Hector. For television, Bremner has appeared in 'The Acid House', 'Ruffian Hearts' and 'Harry Enfield and Chums'.

NIKKI AND TERESA COLLINS (Alex and Susi) are identical twins who play the streetwise daughters of diamond merchant Doug the Head. They turn in convincing performances in their first feature, a coup as there are few female roles in Ritchie's ensemble cast. Apart from their acting debut, the twins have been enjoying successful modelling careers appearing in the Oasis video 'Stand By Me' and a Macleans toothpaste commercial.

SORCHA CUSACK (Mum O'Neil) plays a pivotal role in SNATCH as her son, Brad Pitt's character Mickey, will do anything to make his precious Mam happy. Mum O'Neil has been hardened by life on the road, but has a heart of gold. Cusack has enjoyed a particularly successful stage career with her first outing as Juliet at The Gate, London, in 1979. She returned in 1988 to play Merteuil in 'Les Liaisons Dangereuses' and her stage career has taken her all over London, and indeed the British Isles, as well as to New York and Senegal. Audiences will recognise Cusack for her portrayal of ward sister Kate in the BBC's hit drama 'Casualty'. Other television credits include Jane in 'Jane Eyre', 'Private Affairs' and 'Within These Walls'.

BENICIO DEL TORO (Franky Four Fingers) appears in SNATCH as the man responsible for the first disaster in the diamond delivery. He's an unreformed gambler. Del Toro has given many brilliant performances in a successful and varied film career, which includes 'Swimming with the Sharks', 'The Fan', and 'Fear and Loathing in Las Vegas'. The role for which he has received probably the most critical acclaim is for that of Fenster in the brilliant 'The Usual Suspects'. He has recently finished Michael Mann's 'Drug Wars'.

SAM DOUGLAS (Rosebud) plays Avi's protection Rosebud, who travels everywhere with his boss but despite his fierce loyalty can barely hang on during the rough ride.

Douglas has many impressive feature film credits to his name, which include 'Eyes Wide Shut', 'Fifth Element', 'Hackers', 'Mission Impossible' and 'Batman', and has performed in the Royal National Theatre, London, in 'Raisin in the Sun' and 'The Darker Face of the Earth' as well as other productions across England and America. He will be familiar to television audiences for his performances in 'Kavanagh QC', 'Goodnight Sweetheart', 'Wolverine', 'The Painted Lady' and 'The Dirty Dozen: Next Mission'.

AUSTIN DRAGE (Gypsy Kid 1) is leader of the brat pack of young gypsy kids. He plays a snotty-nosed grub who is bright as a button. Drage has already accumulated some stage and film experience with productions 'Snake in the Grass', 'Waiting for Godot' and 'The Music Man' and a short film aptly named 'The Kid'.

DENNIS FARINA'S (Avi) role launches the film's plot. Avi is the top honcho in New York who'd originally arranged to have the diamond stolen and brought back to him. But his plan spirals out of control. Farina has appeared most recently alongside Ben Affleck in 'Reindeer Games', Claire Daines in 'The Mod Squad' and in 1998's box-office smash 'Saving Private Ryan'. Farina has showcased his dramatic talents in films such as 'Preston Tylk' and 'Manhunter' and his comedic talents in 'That Old Feeling', 'Midnight Run', 'Get Shorty' and 'Out of Sight'. His notable television credits include 'Buddy Faro', 'Crime Story' and 'Miami Vice'. Farina will next be seen in Ed Burns new film 'Sidewalks of New York'.

JASON FLEMYNG (Darren), a former 'Lock Stock' character, returns to Ritchie's side as country ruffian Darren, best friend of Mickey O'Neil. Flemyng has turned in many excellent performances both on the big and small screen. His credits include 'The Hollow Reed', 'Stealing Beauty', 'The James Gang' and 'The Jungle Book'. He won the Best Actor award at the Geneva Film Festival in 1996 for 'Alive and Kicking', has just completed filming 'The Body' in Israel and is currently filming 'Metal Godz' in the US.

ADAM FOGERTY (Gorgeous George) is a gentle giant who looks threatening enough but alas is past his best and doesn't make it through the first round. Adam's career spans both sport and acting – he is an ex-professional boxer and Rugby player and has appeared in numerous TV programmes including 'Coronation Street', 'City Central' and 'Queer as Folk'. His film credits to date include 'Shooting Fish', 'The Power of One', 'Brassed Off' and 'Incognito'.

ALAN FORD (Brick Top) joins Ritchie's line up once again, this time as local kingpin villain Brick Top. Ford is enjoying a prodigious career at the BBC as well as delivering many fine performances for ITV. His feature credits include 'Lock, Stock and Two Smoking Barrels', 'Murder Most Horrid', 'An American Werewolf in London' and 'Buddy's Song'.

ROBBIE GEE (Vinny) plays a small time pawnbroker but big time black man. He's also got a soft spot for his dog. Gee is best known and well loved for his 'Desmonds' character Lee and has also been a regular on the BBC's 'The Real McCoy'. He has performed in the highly acclaimed John Burgess vehicle 'Black Poppies', first shown in London at Stratford East, then at the Royal National Theatre, and most recently for the equivalent BBC television production.

GOLDIE (Bad Boy Lincoln) joins the Vinny/Sol posse as Bad

Boy Lincoln. Goldie has been part of London's hardcore music scene since 1991. His unique creative talent has progressed from being a graffiti writer in his Midlands hometown, to becoming a successful DJ and recording artist with labels such as Reinforced and Synthetic. Under the pseudonym Metalheadz, Goldie made his mark in jungle release and inner city music. 'Timeless' which London Records released in 1994, did well in the charts and demand saw Goldie tour Europe and the US, supporting Björk and cutting another album in collaboration with Noel Gallagher. Thirty-one-year-old Goldie is back in the studio currently doing his own vocals, hosting his Metalheadz sessions at Dingwalls, in London, and looking forward to further feature film work. He enjoyed a successful role in the latest Bond movie 'The World Is Not Enough'. Other projects include starring with David Bowie in 'Everybody Loves Sunshine' and several documentaries.

STEPHEN GRAHAM (Tommy) plays an amateur boxing promoter who is Jason Statham's (Turkish) cheeky sidekick. Both get caught up in this helter-skelter diamond heist. Graham has appeared in several features including 'Blonde Fist', British action thriller 'Downtime' and the Willy Russell screenplay adaptation of 'Stags and Hens', 'Dancin' Thru The Dark'. His theatre credits include stints at The Bush in London, Everyman Liverpool, Bristol Old Vic and performances at Sadler's Wells, London, and the Edinburgh Festival with the NYMT. For television he has enjoyed roles in many of the nation's favourites: 'Coronation Street', 'The Lakes' and 'Heartbeat'.

LENNIE JAMES (Sol) enters the diamond heist as part-owner (with Robbie Gee's Vinny) of a pawnshop and part-time 'gun'. James has enjoyed a varied career, performing extensively throughout London's fringe theatres, The Royal Court, The Tricycle and the Man in the Moon, as well as performances at The Royal National Theatre. His numerous television performances include 'A Touch of Frost', 'Thieftakers' and BBC 1's superbly received 'Cold Feet'. Film credits include Sam Miller's 'Elephant Juice' and 'Among Giants', and Bille August's 'Les Misérables'.

VINNIE JONES (Bullet Tooth Tony) follows his 'Lock, Stock' success as menacing Big Chris, to play Bullet Tooth Tony, a legendary hard man with the markings and reputation to prove it, in Vaughn/Ritchie's latest feature. Jones is a renowned world class footballer who began his professional career at Wimbledon FC, receiving the FA Cup Winner's medal in 1988, playing and captaining some of the finest football teams in Great Britain, as well as being awarded nine caps and captaincy of Wales. A well-loved media star, Jones has hosted his own chat show, made numerous TV and radio appearances, published his own book, and once again delights audiences by lending his 'hard man of football' charm to SNATCH. He recently filmed 'Gone in Sixty Seconds' with Nicolas Cage in America and Jones's next projects take him to Ireland to star in the drama 'No Smoking'. Then back to the UK to play the lead role in the upcoming remake of 'The Mean Machine', originally played by Burt Reynolds and also to be produced by Matthew Vaughn for SKA Films.

BRAD PITT (Mickey O'Neil) takes on the role of the carefree, scrawny Irish gypsy Mickey O'Neil, who's got a knockout punch and more scams than tattoos up his sleeve. Pitt comes fresh from his success in 'Fight Club' and is still remembered for his performance as the beddable hitchhiker in Ridley Scott's 'Thelma and Louise', that first brought worldwide acclaim. Brad has emerged as one of the most prominent actors of his generation, with starring roles in such films as 'Meet Joe Black', 'Seven Years in Tibet', 'Legends of the Fall', 'Seven' and 'Twelve Monkeys'.

MIKE REID (Doug the Head) joins the cast as the cockney cousin to Dennis Farina's character Avi. Though he's a dirty-dealing diamond merchant, he's also a family man who loves his daughters. Reid is well known for his role in the BBC's long running and highly popular series 'EastEnders', where he has played Frank Butcher for the past 12 years.

RADE SERBEDZIJA (Boris the Blade) plays the slick double-crossing Russian who will do whatever it takes to retrieve the diamond. He poses as bodyguard to Benicio Del Toro's Franky Four Fingers. Serbedzija is a widely talented artist with writing and recording credits in addition to his numerous film and theatre performances. He has had a successful European film career, particularly in his native Croatia, and has also been involved in several big studio features which include playing Francois in Warner's 'Mare Largo' and Gibson in Stanley Kubrick's controversial 'Eyes Wide Shut'.

JASON STATHAM (Turkish) is boxing promoter Turkish, the other half of the duo with Stephen Graham's character Tommy. Of the two partners in crime, Turkish is more the man about town, with his fingers in many pies. Statham enjoyed his first feature performance as Bacon, 'the muscle' in 'Lock, Stock and Two Smoking Barrels', after Ritchie spotted him modelling in a Levi's jeans commercial and cast him instantly. As he'll tell you himself, he has a first-hand understanding of being a wheeler-dealer as he used to be a 'dodgy' perfume salesman on London's Oxford Street.

ABOUT THE FILMMAKERS...

MATTHEW VAUGHN (Producer) began his career in film working as Assistant to Simon Fields, Head of Limelight Films in Los Angeles, from which he gained invaluable training in the industry. Upon returning to the UK he worked on various shorts before producing his first feature in 1994, 'The Innocent Sleep'. SNATCH is his second collaboration with director Guy Ritchie after the unequivocal success of 'Lock, Stock and Two Smoking Barrels' which was recently being serialised for television as a spin-off for Channel 4.

GUY RITCHIE (Writer-Director) started his film career as a runner in 1993, then quickly progressed to directing music promos in 1995 for bands and commercials. Ritchie had always been passionate about making films, having been inspired to become a director after watching 'Butch Cassidy and the Sundance Kid' as a child. With the profits from his commercial work, Ritchie invested in writing and making a 20-minute short film 'The Hard Case'. His following project made a 'slightly' bigger impact on the public consciousness and the box office, and now Ritchie's debut feature film 'Lock, Stock and Two Smoking Barrels' is being filmed as a television series.

TIM MAURICE-JONES (Director of Photography) is an accomplished cinematographer with a broad range of experience in music promo's, commercials and features. He has worked with many of the UK's top recording artists including: The Spice Girls, Eternal, Simply Red, Suede, Blur, Take That, and Massive Attack. International artists include: Diana Ross, Björk, Kylie Minogue and Robert Palmer. His commercials work includes worldwide brands such as Levi's, Coors Beer, Smirnoff and Adidas. As well as working on box-office success 'Lock, Stock and Two Smoking Barrels', Maurice-Jones' credits include 'Feast at Midnight' and short films 'If You Loved Me', 'Spook Time' and the award winning 'Weekender'.

HUGO LUCZYC-WYHOWSKI (Production Designer) graduated in 1979 from the University of Newcastle upon Tyne, with a degree in Fine Arts and before long was directing rock videos and commercials. Stephen Frears gave him his first break into feature films when he asked him to design a low budget British film 'My Beautiful Launderette'. He went on to design two further films for Stephen Frears, 'Prick Up Your Ears' and 'Sammy and Rosie Get Laid'. Luczyc-Wyhowski combines his work between the USA and Europe, having designed 'Waterland' for Stephen Gyllenhaal in the Norfolk Fens, 'The Music of Chance' for Phillip Haas in N. Carolina, 'Uncovered' for Jim McBride in Barcelona and 'Cousin Bette' for Des MacAnuff in France. More recently he has designed Jex Butterworth's 'Mojo', Gary Oldman's acclaimed directorial debut 'Nil By Mouth' and Daisy Mayer's 'Madeline' for TriStar Pictures.

VERITY HAWKES (Costume Designer) Verity Hawkes is an accomplished costume designer boasting a variety of experience, encompassing both commercial work and films. She graduated from the Wimbledon School of Art in 1989 with a BA Hons in Theatre Design. Her film credits include 'Cold Enough For Snow', 'If You Loved Me' and the short film 'Tube Tales', directed by a host of well-known names such as Ewan McGregor and Jude Law.

LUCINDA SYSON (Casting Director) has an impressive reputation that extends from casting in the UK to France,

Spain, Portugal, India and Argentina. She was responsible for securing the American contingent in SNATCH – Brad Pitt, Benicio Del Toro, Dennis Farina – as well as casting the charismatic posse of British characters. Other film credits include 'The Visitors', 'Hotel Splendide', 'The Messenger – Joan of Arc', 'Entrapment' and 'The Fifth Element'. Syson was also joint Casting Director on 'Everafter' and 'The Thirteenth Warrior', and Associate Casting Director for 'Seven Years in Tibet'. She is a member of the Casting Directors Guild (UK) and has cast several successful commercials.

FAE HAMMOND (Make-up Designer) is a versatile and widely experienced make-up and hair designer for both feature films and television. Before working on SNATCH, (in which she also helped to design and paint freehand Pitt's remarkable tattoos), Hammond has worked on many notable film productions such as 'The Wrong Blond', 'Ravenous', 'Lost in Space', 'Nil by Mouth', 'Heart of Darkness' and 'The Young Americans'. She has acquired 11 years of training at the BBC and has worked for Granada and Channel 4 in the UK. Her TV credits include 'The New Adventures of Robin Hood', 'Young Indiana Jones Chronicles', 'Rick Mayall Presents the Big One', 'Pig Boy', and 'Body Beautiful'. Hammond's next project is 'The Knight's Tale', a Columbia picture to be shot in Prague.

JON HARRIS (Editor) Jon Harris has worked as an editor for a variety of projects stretching from music videos to documentaries and dramas to movie trailers. His short film credits include 'Occasional'; 'The Second Death' and the 1999 Oscar nominated short film drama 'Strong Holiday Romance'. Harris has also worked as an Assistant Editor on 'When Saturday Comes' and on Joseph Conrad's 'The Secret Agent'. SNATCH is Harris's first feature as an Editor.

JOHN MURPHY (Film Composer) is among Britain's most prominent film composers. Murphy was originally half of the production team with David Hughes and they first collaborated as composers seven years ago with the award-winning score for Brit-hit 'Leon The Pig Farmer'. They then went on to produce the scores for seventeen feature films with credits including 'Lock, Stock and Two Smoking Barrels', 'The Bachelor' (Chris O'Donnell and Rene Zellweger), 'Tube Tales' ('Horny' by Stephen Hopkins) and 'Shiny New Enemies' (Salma Hayek, Jeff Goldblum). Murphy is currently working on 'The Fridge' starring Catherine Deneuve and Natasha Leone.

CAST (in alphabetical order)

Tyrone .... Ade
Neil .... William Beck
Errol .... Andy Beckwith
Mullet .... Ewen Bremner
Gary .... Jason Buckham
Liam .... Mickey Cantwell
Alex .... Nikki Collins
Susi .... Teena Collins
MC .... Charles Cork
Horrible Man .... James Cunningham
Mum O'Neil .... Sorcha Cusack
Jack the All Seeing Eye .... Mickey Dee
Franky Four Fingers .... Benicio Del Toro
Rosebud .... Sam Douglas
Avi .... Dennis Farina
Darren .... Jason Flemyng
Gorgeous George .... Adam Fogerty
Brick Top .... Alan Ford
Vinny .... Robbie Gee
Bad Boy Lincoln .... Goldie
Tommy .... Stephen Graham
Reuben .... Sid Hoare
Referee .... Ronnie Isaac
Sol .... Lennie James
Bullet Tooth Tony .... Vinnie Jones
Michael .... Chuck Julian
John .... Dave Legeno
Avi's Colleague .... Eric Meyers
Charlie .... Jason Ninh Cao
Patrick .... Paul O'Boyle
Mickey O'Neil .... Brad Pitt
Doug the Head .... Mike Reid

Paulie	Jimmy Roussounis
Pauline	Sidney Sedin
Boris the Blade	Rade Sherbedgia
Turkish	Jason Stratham
Bomber Harris	Trevor Steedman
Himy	Yuri Stepanov
Sausage Charlie	Peter Szakacs
Salt Peter	John Taheny
Mad First Willy	Mick Theo
John the Gun	Andy Till
The Russian	Velibor Topic
Horace 'Good Night' Anderson	Scott Welch
Gypsy Men	Michael Hughes
	Liam McMahon
	Joe Williams
Gypsy Kids	Austin Drage
	Liam Donaghy
	Michael Greene
Brick Top's Henchmen	John Farnell
	Shaun Pearson
	Dean Smith
	Roy Snell
Policemen	Tim Faraday
	Andrew Shield

CREW

Writer/ Director	Guy Ritchie
Producer	Matthew Vaughn
Executive Producers	Stephen Marks
	Angad Paul
	Peter Morton
	Steve Tisch
	Trudi Styler

Associate Producers ....Sebastian Pearson
                                                      Taha Ali Reza
Co-producer .... Michael Dreyer
Production Manager .... Adam Bohling
Production Co-ordinator .... Emma Pike
Production Assistant .... Debbie Ninnis
Production Runner .... Simon Nixon
Director's Assistant ....Dan Cadan
Development .... Kate Myers
SKA PA .... Nicole Gregory
2nd Assistant Director .... Dan Toland
Director of Photography .... Tim Maurice-Jones
Camera Operator .... Peter Wignall
Focus Puller .... Stuart Graham
Grip .... Terry Williams
Casting Director .... Lucinda Syson
Casting Assistant .... Emma Engers
Location Manager .... Pat Karam
Production Runner .... Paul Ettinger
Production Accountant .... Susan Merritt
Account Assistant .... Stephen Naulls
Production Designer .... Hugo Luczyc-Wyhowski
Art Director .... Julie Philpott
Assistant Art Director .... Martin Foley
Assistant Art Director .... Verena Khan
Props Buyer .... Linda Wilson
lst Assistant Director .... David Reid
Assistant Location Manager .... Giles Edleston
Make-up Designer .... Fae Hammond
Make-up Artist .... Pebbles
Sound Mixer .... Simon Hayes
Boom Operator .... Arthur Turner
Special Effects Supervisor .... Ken Lailey

SNATCH

by
Guy Ritchie

Intro.   INT. DOUG'S OFFICE – DAY

FADE UP FROM BLACK

We start on the back of a man's head (first titles begin). The camera pans up to reveal he's on one side of a desk in a dark room with his back to us. On the other side are Turkish and Tommy. Turkish is sitting in quiet contemplation, Tommy is chewing gum, glancing around and distracted by a fly. What they are waiting for, we don't know. We hear Turkish's V/O.

                    TURKISH (V/O)
My name is Turkish, funny name for an Englishman I know. My parents to be were on the same plane when it crashed, that's how they met. They named me after the name of the plane, not many people are named after a plane crash. That's Tommy, he tells people he was named after a gun, but I know he was named after a famous nineteenth century ballet dancer. Known him for as long as I can remember. He's my partner, doesn't mean we hold hands or take windy walks, but what it really means is I try to keep him out of as much trouble as he inflicts on me. I give him a hard time, keeps him in check. But really he's like my brother. What do I know about diamonds? I'm a boxing promoter. I was a happy boxing promoter until a week ago and then... what do I know about diamonds? Don't they come from Antwerp?

FADE TO BLACK

24

INT. FOYER – DAY

> JOSEPH (over black)
> Himey would you listen to this?

On a security CCTV camera we are looking at four Hasidic
Jews entering a building. They are identically dressed in
black hats, black suits, black overcoats and they have curly
wurly beards and fat tummies. One is particularly fat,
bespectacled and American. His name is Mutti and he is
talking.

MAIN TITLES begin over monitors.

CAPTION: ANTWERP

> HIMY
> Do we have a choice?

> MUTTI
> A lot of it wasn't meant to be taken literally.

They walk up to a security desk and walk through a security
arch. Three of them walk through without a blip until Mutti
goes through. One of the guards stops him.

> GUARD (in Belgian)
> Stop.

He whips out a hand metal detector and runs it over Mutti's
body.

> MUTTI
> It's a nice story, Adam and Eve, it's bound with moral

fibre, but asking a grown man to believe it, well...

It appears that Mutti's belt has triggered the alarm off. It beeps.

GUARD (gesturing)
What is it?

Mutti does not move or respond.

GUARD
Well, what is it?

Mutti pulls his belt up.

MUTTI
What do you want I should do, drop my pants?

GUARD
OK go through.

The security guards wave them on to the lift. They continue talking.

EXT. LIFT – DAY

We pick them up on another security camera. We will follow their journey into the lift and through the building on various CCTV monitors – panning from one to the next, panning up etc.

JOSEPH
Mutti it's just that a story

MUTTI

The Catholic religion is based on a mistranslation…

HIMY

Oh enough already. Reuben will you say something?

MUTTI

…Listen to this, are you busy, I'll tell you the whole
story. The Septuagint scholars mistranslated the
Hebrew word for 'young woman' into the Greek word
for 'virgin'. It was an easy mistake to make because
there was only a subtle difference in the spelling…

They all enter the lift. New CCTV camera on all of them in
the lift.

MUTTI

…So they came up with the prophecy 'behold a virgin
shall conceive and bear us a son'. You understand this:
it was the word virgin that caught people's attention.
It's not every day a virgin conceives and bears a son.

INT. VARIOUS CORRIDORS – DAY

Various security cameras pick them up walking
through corridors.

MUTTI

Well, leave that for a couple of hundred years to stew
and the next thing you know…you have the holy
Catholic church.

JOSEPH

Oi vay. What are you saying?

                    MUTTI
     I'm saying just cos it's written, doesn't make it so.
     Gives them hope. It's not really important whether it's
     fact or fiction, people like to believe.

                    HIMY
     I don't want to hear anymore.

The four men come to a stop outside a door.
Mutti presses a buzzer.

                    HIMY (cont'd)
     Anyway, who is it that we are seeing?

                    MUTTI
     Michael.

          VOICE FROM INTERCOM
     Hello.

               MUTTI (in Hebrew)
     Hello.

          VOICE FROM INTERCOM
     Who's that?

                    MUTTI
     Mutti.

The camera pans from the four men on the monitor into the
room (we go from the black and white of the CCTV
monitor to the colour of real life in the room).

> MICHAEL (off-camera, excited)
> Rudd, Rudd let them in, please.

The four men enter through the door and pass the security guard. He's sitting in front of the CCTV monitors that have shown us their journey upstairs.

> MICHAEL (off-camera)
> Ruddi, Rudd, Rudd, let them through.

INT. BACK ROOM DIAMOND DEALERS – DAY

Michael comes to greet them.

> MUTTI (off camera)
> Michael.

> MICHAEL
> Mutti, you have kept us waiting for half an hour. Are you trying to give me heartburn?

Michael pauses.

> MICHAEL (cont'd)
> Mutti. Mutti?

Michael starts to frown. We cut back to Mutti. He rips open his shirt and underneath he is harbouring a selection of guns, all three of the other men grab the weapons.
They start shouting, hitting employees. It's a raid. The scene is cut down to a few valuable relevant moments, diamonds being collected up. It's a sequence of shots – freeze frames, camera spins, stop motion shots, disconnected words repeated for effect.

FINAL MAIN TITLES also appear. Finally we stop on Michael and Mutti face to face.

> MUTTI (to Michael)
> Where is the stone?

Michael quivers. Mutti picks up an employee off the floor, holding him roughly.

> MUTTI (to Michael)
> Where is the stone?

Mutti pistol whips the employee.

> MUTTI (to Michael, drawling now)
> Where is the stone?

Again, Mutti pistol whips the employee who falls to the floor. Mutti points the gun at Michael.

> MUTTI
> Michael, where is the stone?

Michael quivers. His eyes widen.

Cut to a shot of a large diamond.

INT. VAN – DAY

The four 'Jews' are now in a van peeling off the Hasidic outfits – beards, clothes etc. They are all lean, fit, serious-looking men.

Mutti (aka Franky Four Fingers) holds up the stone.
The camera tracks in to the stone.

CUT TO: MUSIC, A CLOSE-UP OF THE DIAMOND.
MIX TO: AVI LOOKING AT THE STONE THROUGH A
MAGNIFYING GLASS. CUT TO: MONTAGE
INVOLVING ALL THE CHARACTERS IN THE FILM,
WE MOVE FROM ONE CHARACTER TO THE NEXT,
THROUGH PASSING THE DIAMOND, CASH, GOLD,
GUNS ETC. ONE SHOT SEAMLESSLY INTO
ANOTHER SHOT AND SET UP. THIS GOES ON FOR
THE DURATION OF THE CREDITS.
CUT BACK TO: C/U DIAMOND

Franky Four Fingers kisses the diamond, opens a fancy case
and puts it into a compartment in the case and shuts it
firmly. Reuben aka 'the Russian' is next to him and watches
him.

RUSSIAN
When does your plane leave?

FRANKY FOUR FINGERS
Twenty minutes.

RUSSIAN
Give me your gun.

FRANKY FOUR FINGERS opens the gun, drops the bullets
on to the floor, and hands it to the Russian.

RUSSIAN
When you get to London, if you want a gun, call this
number.

Franky takes the paper, looks at it and repeats the name.

> FRANKY FOUR FINGERS
> Boris?

> RUSSIAN
> Boris. He can get you anything you need.

The Russian spins the gun chamber...

EXT. TURKISH'S BACK ALLEY MAKESHIFT BOXING
RING – DAY

CAPTION: LONDON

...And a whip pan shot takes us into this boxing ring. Meet
TURKISH and TOMMY, boxing promoters. They are both
watching their boxer Gorgeous George go through his paces.
He's a rough-looking bastard, he's massive and extremely
ugly. Gorgeous is punching a heavy punch bag. The sound
that emanates is disturbing, and Tommy is distracted.

> TOMMY
> Is he allowed to do that?

> TURKISH
> It's an unlicensed boxing match Tommy, not a tickling
> competition. These lads are out to hurt each other.
> What's happening with those sausages, Charlie?

Turkish turns to see the remnants of a caravan where they
keep the training gear and administration for the fights.
There is a barbecue blazing and an old boy turning sausages.

CHARLIE

Two minutes, Turkish.

TURKISH

Look at that.

He looks at the caravan again and sighs; it is quite pitiful.

TURKISH (cont'd)

How am I supposed to run this thing from that? We're gonna need a proper office. I want a new one Tommy, and you're going to buy it for me.

TOMMY

Why me?

TURKISH

Well, you know about caravans.

TOMMY

How's that?

TURKISH

You spent a summer in one. Which means you know more than me. And I don't want to have my pants pulled down over the price.

TOMMY

What's wrong with this one?

Turning back to Tommy and ascending the steps into his 'I have seen better days' caravan, the door comes off the hinges as Turkish tries to open it.

TURKISH

Oh nothing, Tommy, it's tip-top, it's just I'm not sure about the colour.

He passes Tommy a piece of paper.

TURKISH (cont'd)

Here, it's all arranged, you just gotta pick it up. Here's an address.

Tommy looks at the address and frowns.

TOMMY

It's a campsite.

Turkish passes Tommy an envelope. Turkish is now holding a pint of milk and drinking it.

TURKISH (cont'd)

You've got ten grand and it would be nice to see change. What's happening with them sausages, Charlie?

CHARLIE

Five minutes, Turkish.

TURKISH

It was two minutes, five minutes ago!

TOMMY

Well they ain't pikeys are they? I fuckin' hate pikeys.

Tommy and Turkish walk away from the caravan.

TURKISH
You're a sensitive boy, ain't ya Tommy?

He is distracted by the bulge in Tommy's trouser front.

TURKISH (cont'd)
Fuck me, hold tight, what's that?

TOMMY
It's me belt, Turkish.

Turkish looks towards Tommy's belt.

TURKISH
No, Tommy, there's a gun in your trousers. What is a
gun doing in your trousers?

TOMMY
It's for protection.

TURKISH
Protection from what, 'zee Germans'? What's to stop it
blowing your bollocks off every time you sit down?
Where did you get it?

Turkish pulls the gun out of Tommy's front.

TOMMY
Boris the Blade.

TURKISH
You mean Boris the sneaky fucking Russian. It's a bit
heavy innit?

He spins the gun chamber and we whip pan to …

INT. LONDON – AMUSEMENT ARCADE – BACK
OFFICE – DAY

CAPTION: EARLIER

Tommy is sitting at a desk toying with a heavy-looking
revolver, spinning the gun chamber. In front of him on the
desk are various other weapons. Meet BORIS THE BLADE, a
local arms dealer, who's sitting on the other side of the desk.

> BORIS
> Heavy is good. Heavy is reliable. If it doesn't work you
> can always hit him with it.

> TURKISH (V/O over freeze of Boris)
> Boris the Blade or Boris the Bullet Dodger, as bent as the
> Soviet sickle and as hard as the hammer that crosses it.
> Apparently it's just impossible to kill the bastard.

Tommy practises a couple of gun-slinging manoeuvres. He's
impressed. At that moment the door opens and in walks
GORGEOUS GEORGE.

> TURKISH (V/O over above)
> Back to my partner Tommy. Tommy runs the other
> business, the slot machines which keeps the rain off
> our heads and the gloves on Gorgeous's hands.
> However, Tommy is a little preoccupied with
> protection at present.

> TOMMY
> All right, I'll take it.

INT. BRICK TOP'S BOXING RING – DAY

BRICK TOP (aka MR PULFORD) is a slight but dodgy looking fella. He is observing two men boxing. He's with TWO HENCHMEN, ERROL and JOHN, and TWO EMPLOYEES, LIAM and GARY.

> TURKISH (V/O cont'd)
> There is a reason for Tommy's new-found enthusiasm for firearms. Sooner or later in the unlicensed boxing world you're going to have to deal with that reason: Brick Top.

And as he speaks we draw back to see Brick Top.

> BRICK TOP
> If that's not worth a bet I don't know what is.

He's talking to LIAM and GARY, the employees.

> BRICK TOP (cont'd)
> He doesn't look bad does he?

> GARY
> Oh no, Mr Pulford, he looks great, he'll do you proud, governor.

> BRICK TOP
> Do you reckon that's what people should do for me, do you Gary, do me proud?

> GARY
> That's what you deserve Mr Pulford.

BRICK TOP

Pull your tongue out of my arsehole Gary. Dogs do
that, and you're not a dog, are you Gary?

Gary's taken aback by the change in tone.

GARY

Err, no, I'm not.

BRICK TOP

However, you do have all of the characteristics of a
dog, Gary – all except loyalty.

There is a definite change in temperature. Once again
Turkish's V/O cuts in and runs over a freeze frame of Brick
Top as he walks away from the ring and Gary and Liam.
Then a montage of shots into freeze – a stun gun is put to
Gary's side, a plastic bag is produced and handed to Liam,
who moves forward and a roll of tape is measured out.

TURKISH (V/O over above)

It's rumoured that Brick Top's favourite means of
despatch involves a stun gun, a plastic bag, a roll of
tape and a pack of hungry pigs.

CUT BACK TO: Brick Top in action again.

BRICK TOP

You're a ruthless little cunt Liam, I'll give you that.

Brick Top walks away at this point.

BRICK TOP (cont'd)

But I got no time for grasses.

Liam panics. John whips another plastic bag over his head.

> BRICK TOP (cont'd)
> Feed 'em to the pigs, Errol.

With a short beat Brick Top turns to his fighters again.

> BRICK TOP (cont'd)
> What the fuck are you two looking at?

CUT TO: the shocked boxers in the ring.

INT. PIG FARM – NIGHT

> TURKISH (V/O)
> If you're going to deal with him you've just got to make sure you don't end up owing him. Because then you're in his debt, which means you're in his pocket, and once you're in that you ain't ever coming out.

Turkish and Tommy take a walk with Brick Top and his henchmen through his pig farm. Brick Top periodically feeds the pigs with grain.

> BRICK TOP
> I hear he's a good fighter, so I'm gonna use him but I'll be doing you a favour, boy.

> TURKISH (V/O)
> What he means is I'm doing him a favour because everybody knows nobody takes a dive in my fights unlike his.

BRICK TOP
Here Errol, I don't think he likes me. You don't like me
do ya boy?

TURKISH
I don't know what you mean.

TURKISH (V/O)
I do know I can't wait to get out of here. Fuck me it
stinks.

BRICK TOP
I like my fights to finish prompt so we can get the
punters out before the authorities find out. Now play
your cards right and I'll sort you out.

TURKISH (V/O)
You can sort me out by showing me out. It's hard
enough to make a living in the boxing world so every
now and then you've got to do something that might
not agree with your principles. Basically, you have to
forget you've got any.

TOMMY
Are they Lancashire pigs?

BRICK TOP
Who the fuck's talking to you, boy?

TURKISH (V/O)
Oh yeah, Tommy, Brick Top loves Tommy.

BRICK TOP
Now don't let me down, you don't want to let me

down, do ya boy?

> TURKISH
> See you ringside.

INT. BORIS'S HOUSE (LONDON)/RUSSIAN'S HOUSE
(ANTWERP) – SPLITSCREEN – DAY

They are both on the phone, subtitled. Boris speaks Russian.
He is pretty relaxed.

SPLITSCREEN

> RUSSIAN
> Boris, Franky Fuckin' Four Fingers has a diamond the
> size of a fist. I have told you it is in the briefcase
> connected to his arm. I send him to you to buy a gun.
> What more do you want me to do? Hit him for you?
> And don't you hit him either. Americans can't know it
> was Russian. It will come back to me.

> BORIS (in Russian)
> So, what should I do?

Boris seems pretty relaxed in his response. The Russian's
pretty annoyed.

CAPTIONS: ANTWERP/LONDON

> RUSSIAN
> Boris, you're my brother so think like my brother! Get
> somebody else to steal that fuckin' stone. I just don't
> want it getting back to me and don't you have him killed
> Boris. It will raise suspicion so don't use idiots for the

job. He's going to stay in London only for a couple of days before he goes to New York so move quick OK?

Boris sits down with a cup of tea.

> BORIS (in Russian)
> It's OK, I know a couple of guys.

> RUSSIAN
> One more thing. It might help. He loves to gamble.

INT. NEW YORK OFFICE – DAY

CAPTION: NEW YORK

Meet AVI. On the phone. Streetwise NY diamond dealer. He catches a coin.

> AVI
> Eighty-six carats?

INT. TAILORS/INT. NEW YORK OFFICE – DAY/CONTINUOUS

CAPTION: LONDON

Franky's in London being fitted at the tailors, on the phone to Avi in New York.

> FRANKY FOUR FINGERS
> Brilliant cut, beautiful make, clean, no fluorescence, a beautiful stone.

                           AVI

You're a good boy Franky, a good boy and you did a
real good job. Now, when do you get back?

                  FRANKY FOUR FINGERS

I gotta move the melées and two grainers here, and get
a better price. A couple of days.

                           AVI

Talk to my cousin Dougie.

                  FRANKY FOUR FINGERS

Doug the Head?

                           AVI

Yeah, Doug the Head. And … Franky –

                  FRANKY FOUR FINGERS

And what?

                           AVI

Stay out of those casinos.

CUT TO: MONTAGE OF FRANKY AND GAMBLING
STILLS. THEN BACK TO AVI IN NEW YORK.

                      AVI (cont'd)

You did a good job Bubbi, don't go screwing it up.

                  FRANKY FOUR FINGERS

I hear ya, Avi. I'll see ya, Avi.

The phone goes down and Avi looks up at two employees –
including ROSEBUD, his henchman.

                         AVI
Eighty-six carats.

                       ROSEBUD
Where?

                         AVI
London.

                       ROSEBUD
London?

                         AVI
London.

                    AVI'S COLLEAGUE
London?

                         AVI
Yes, London. You know, fish 'n' chips, cup o' tea, bad
food, worse weather, Mary fuckin' Poppins. London.

INT. PUB – DAY

CAPTION: BACK IN LONDON

DOUG THE HEAD is a seemingly east London Jew, about
forty-five, almost completely bald and proud of it. He is
inspecting a Rolex watch.

                        DOUG
No, Paulie, that ain't for me.

Doug finishes his drink and waits for his sandwich.

                    TURKISH (V/O)
That's Doug the Head. Everybody knows Doug the
Head. If it's stones and it's stolen Doug's the man to
speak to. Pretends he's Jewish. Wishes he was Jewish.
Even tells his family they're Jewish but he's about as
Jewish as he is a fuckin' monkey. He thinks it's good
for business, and in the diamond business...

Doug leaves the pub with his sandwich and his mobile
phone starts to ring.

INT. NEW YORK OFFICE – DAY/EXT. HATTON
GARDEN, LONDON

                        AVI
Doug the Head?

                    TURKISH (V/O)
...It is good for business.

                       DOUG
Avi.

                        AVI
He'll be there today. Take care of him will ya?

                       DOUG
Avi, you know I won't buy shtrops.

                        AVI
He isn't selling shtrops. (Then to an employee in the
office.) Smaller, make it smaller.

                        52

                    DOUG

What do you take me for? This is England, we play by
the rules. Listen to me, if the stones are kosher then I'll
buy them, won't I? Now, if you'll excuse me, it's my
lunch time. Bye.

He hangs up and stops outside his shop where there are
some young Jewish boys loitering.

                  JEWISH KID
Yeah man.

                    DOUG
What are you doing here?

                  JEWISH KID
It's a free country, innit?

                    DOUG
Well it ain't a free shop is it, so fuck off!

INT. JEWELLERY SHOP – DAY

He walks into his shop. Behind the counter is a girl.

                DOUG (cont'd)
I wanna see you two girls up in my office. I've just had
Cousin Avi on the phone. You know you've got to go
out and see him...

                    ALEX
Yeah, Dad, you told us.

DOUG

He's a big mucker in New York.

Girl identical to Alex stands up – she was under the counter.

SUSI

Yeah, Dad, you told us.

DOUG

I want to see you two girls up in my office.

SUSI/ALEX

Yeah, Dad, you told us!

Doug wearily walks away to his office.

INT. BORIS'S HOUSE – DAY

Boris spinning the gun chamber. He has another customer.

BORIS

The weight is a sign of reliability. I always go for
reliability.

Boris is showing Franky a large pistol.

FRANKY FOUR FINGERS

I'll take it. How much do you want for it?

BORIS

Nothing.

Pause.

FRANKY FOUR FINGERS
OK, so what do you want for it?

BORIS
I want you to do something for me.

Franky nods for him to go on.

FRANKY FOUR FINGERS
Hmmmm.

BORIS
There's a fight in a couple of days.

FRANKY FOUR FINGERS
What kind of a fight?

BORIS
Unlicensed boxing. There's a bookie's I know that will take bets.

FRANKY FOUR FINGERS
Aha.

CUT TO: MONTAGE OF FRANKY AND GAMBLING STILLS.

BORIS
If you place one down for me, we will call it quits.

FRANKY FOUR FINGERS
Why don't you put it down yourself?

BORIS

Well, there is not too many bookies that take those
kind of bets, and I already have an outstanding debt
with the house. I know something most don't.

FRANKY FOUR FINGERS

So, nu, what do you know?

INT. TOMMY'S CAR/CAMPSITE – DAY

Georgeous George is driving down a country lane with
Tommy in the passenger seat.

GORGEOUS GEORGE

It's a campsite. A pikey campsite.

TOMMY

Ten points.

GORGEOUS GEORGE

What we doing here?

TOMMY

We're buying a caravan.

GORGEOUS GEORGE

Off a pack of fucking pikeys? What's wrong with you?
This will get messy.

TOMMY

Not if you're here.

GORGEOUS GEORGE
Ohh, you bastard. I fuckin' hate pikeys.

EXT. CARAVAN CAMPSITE – DAY

They arrive in the campsite and the car is immediately
surrounded by kids. The kids (most of whom are on bikes)
speak with a sort of Anglo-Irish mix that sounds as rough as
the kids look.

KID 1
That's a flash car Mister.

TOMMY
Not as flash as your bike though is it?

KID 1
Who are you looking for?

TOMMY
Mr O'Neil.

Children are milling around the car and Gorgeous George
winds down his window.

KID 1
Do you want me to go and get him?

TOMMY
That's a good lad.

GORGEOUS GEORGE
(to the children outside his car window)
Piss off.

Meanwhile, Tommy is still waiting for the kid to go and find Mr O'Neil.

> TOMMY
> Well are you going to go and get him for me ?

> KID 1
> Yeah.

There is another pause...

> TOMMY
> Well, what you waiting for?

> KID 1
> The five quid you're going to pay me.

Chuckling.

> TOMMY
> Oh fuck off, I'll find him meself.

> KID 1
> Two-fifty.

> TOMMY
> You can have a quid.

> KID 1
> Oh, you're a real tight fucker, aren't ya?

> TURKISH (V/O)
> Now there is a problem with pikeys or gypsies...

A MAN shouts from the background. He's a young fella with a hard but friendly face (when he smiles). He's covered in grease and facial hair, and his trousers are done up with string. This is Mickey O'Neil.

> MICKEY
> What are you doing, Paul? Get out of the way, boy.

> TURKISH (V/O cont'd)
> ...You can't really understand much of what is being said.

> MICKEY
> Are you Tommy? Have you come about the caravan?

> TOMMY
> Mr O'Neil?

Mickey comes up to the car.

> MICKEY
> Fuck man, call me Mickey.

> TURKISH (V/O cont'd)
> ...It's not Irish, it's not English...

> TOMMY
> How are ya?

> MICKEY
> The weather is being kind to us, but the horses you know.

> TURKISH (V/O cont'd)
> ...it's just, well, it's just pikey.

Gorgeous George steps out of the car. Mickey takes a step back.

>MICKEY
>
>Fuck me, would you look at the size of him. How big are you? Hey kids, how big is he?

>KID 2
>
>He's a big man, that's for sure.

>MICKEY
>
>Hey Mam, come and look at the size of this fella.

Mickey's mum comes out to see.

>MICKEY (cont'd)
>
>I bet you can box a little, can't you sir? You look like a boxer. (Starts to feint and punch.)

>MUM O'NEIL
>
>Get out of the way Mickey, see if the fellas would like a drink.

>TOMMY
>
>Oh, I could murder one.

>MUM O'NEIL
>
>There'll be no murdering done around here, I don't mind telling ya.

One of the kids is furtively searching Georgeous George's pocket. The kid is grabbed by Mickey.

MICKEY

Get your hand out of there you rascal, you cheeky little
shite.

Mickey shoos the kid away.

MICKEY (cont'd)

Cup of tea for the big fella.

MUM O'NEIL

Don't be silly Mickey, offer the man a proper drink, like.
Mickey shadow boxes with one of the kids while Tommy
walks with Mrs O'Neil to her caravan.

MUM O'NEIL

Is the big fella not coming with us?

TOMMY

No he's minding the car.

MUM O'NEIL

What does he think we are, thieves.

TOMMY

Oh no, nothing like that Mrs O'Neil, he just likes
looking after cars.

Mickey is now on the steps of the caravan. There are dogs
milling around.

MICKEY

Good dogs, do you like dogs?

                    TOMMY

Dags?

                    MICKEY

What?

                    MUM O'NEIL

Yeah, dogs.

                    MICKEY

Yeah, dogs. Do you like dogs?

                    TOMMY

Oh, dogs. Sure I like dags. I like caravans more.

                    MICKEY

Hmmm.

                    MUM O'NEIL

You're very welcome

Mrs O'Neil pushes him up the steps into the caravan.

EXT. CARAVAN CAMPSITE – DAY

Gorgeous George fastens the caravan to the back of their car
while various rough looking gypsy men watch, including
Darren and Patrick, Mickey's sidekicks.

                    TURKISH (V/O)

Now pikeys are well known for their skills of
negotiations in business. It's part of the reason they talk
like they do so you can't follow what's being said. But if
Tommy can get the caravan for less than the price
asked, on his return there'll be a ice-cream waiting.

Georgeous George gets in the car next to Tommy and a dog.

                    MICKEY
          Good dog, a good family. Hold on to him tight, he'll
          get a little homesick for a while but he'll get over it. See
          you later, lads. See you, boss.

Tommy has a dog that looks distressed about leaving.
Mickey sitting next to him.

                    TOMMY
          All right Mickey, laters.

INT. TOMMY'S CAR – DAY

                    TOMMY (cont'd)
          I don't see what all the fuss is about. They aren't bad
          fellas.

Just then the wheels of the caravan come straight off and the
caravan is dragged until the car comes to a sudden stop. The
dog jumps out the window and goes bounding back to the
campsite.

EXT. CARAVAN CAMPSITE – DAY

Tommy and Gorgeous are talking to Mickey, Darren,
Patrick and various other Irish gypsies outside the caravan.
The atmosphere is tense.

                    MICKEY
          The deal was you bought it how you saw it. Now look,
          I'm gonna help ya as much as I'm gonna help ya. You
          see that car, I suggest you use it before you're not

welcome anymore.

There is a silence for a while. The atmosphere has gone more than frosty.

GORGEOUS GEORGE

I think...

Interrupted.

MICKEY

You should fuck off now while you've still got the legs to carry ya.

GORGEOUS GEORGE

Nobody –

Interrupted.

MICKEY

Nobody brings a fella the size of you unless they are trying to say something without talking, right boy?

TOMMY (pacifying)

Sorry Mickey, just give us our money back and you can keep your caravan.

MICKEY

Why the fuck do I want a caravan that's got no fuckin' wheels?

Gorgeous George steps forward. Mickey gets up in answer – dogs bark, everyone gets ready to fight.

MICKEY (cont'd)
Where the fuck do you think you're going? You want
to settle this with a fight?

MUM O'NEIL
(interrupting and shouting)
Over my dead body. Go on, go on …

Mrs O'Neil pushes Gorgeous away.

MICKEY
(trying to usher her away)
Mam, mam.

Mickey's mum is getting upset which upsets Mickey.

MRS O'NEIL
I'll not have you fighting, Mickey, you know what
happens when you fight.

MICKEY
OK, Mam, OK. You need to sit down.

We see Mickey's mum being led into her caravan by Darren.
Mickey looks genuinely concerned for his mum.

MICKEY
For fuck's sake.

Pause…as Mickey waits for her to be well gone.

MICKEY (cont'd)
You want the money, I'll fuck ya. I'll fight you for it,
you and me.

Gorgeous George looks quizzical.

INT. STABLE – DAY

It looks a bit ridiculous, Mickey is dwarfed by comparison.
Gorgeous George takes two sneaky swipes. Mickey's head is
whipped round in various directions. He falls to the floor,
wiping blood from his nose.

>   MICKEY
>   So that's the kind of fight it's gonna be.

>   GORGEOUS GEORGE
>   You want to stay down.

Gorgeous George lunges and grabs Mickey by the throat
and groin, picks him up like a sack of spuds and throws him
against the wire mesh fence. Gorgeous kicks him as he lies
on the floor.

>   GEORGEOUS GEORGE (cont'd)
>   You wanna stay down.

George walks away. Mickey jumps up.The crowd cheers.
With his back to George, Mickey takes his jacket off and
begins to limber up.

>   GEORGEOUS GEORGE
>   Get back down. Fucking stay down. I promise you that
>   you want to stay down.

Mickey ignores this and continues to pace.

MICKEY
Deadly kick for a fat fuck, d'you know that?

GORGEOUS GEORGE
You cheeky bastard!

The big fella grabs him and puts him in a headlock and
charges him into the wooden stable gate wall. There is a
terrible noise. Mickey lies still. His boys help Mickey up.
All of a sudden he starts jumping up and down like he's
warming up, stretching.

GORGEOUS GEORGE (cont'd)
Get back down or you will not be coming up next
time.

Mickey begins to limber up and throw out a couple of
shadow punches.

GORGEOUS GEORGE (cont'd)
Oh bollocks to yous, this is sick. I'm out of here.

Mickey takes off his shirt. This reveals a heavily tattooed
and scarred torso, and underneath these embellishments is
a physique that warrants some respect.

MICKEY
You're not going anywher...You'll stay until the job's
done.

Gorgeous George looks at him and rushes forward. Mickey
kisses his pendant for luck and catches the big man under
the jaw.

CUT TO BLACK

FADE IN: We see Gorgeous George lying on the floor flat out, eyes open with a head the size of a water melon. There's a lot of activity going on around the body on the floor. Their mouths are open but we can't hear what they are saying. All we can hear is Turkish's voice-over and the music.

> TURKISH (V/O)
> It turns out that the sweet-talking, tattoo-sporting pikey was a gypsy bare-knuckle boxing champion which makes him harder than a coffin nail.

Cut to a nervous looking, tearful Tommy, while Darren and Patrick argue either side of him.

> TURKISH (V/O cont'd)
> Right now that's the last thing on Tommy's mind. If Gorgeous doesn't wake up in the next few minutes Tommy'll know he'll be buried with him. Why would the gypsies want to go to the trouble of explaining why a man died in their campsite? Not when they can bury the pair of them and just move camp. It's not like they've got Social Security numbers, is it? Tommy, the tit, is praying and if he isn't, he fuckin' should be.

FADE TO BLACK

EXT. STREET OUTSIDE DOUG'S
OFFICE/PAWNBROKER'S – DAY

Meet Vinny, tall black guy who is walking a young rotund dog. The dog tries to sniff a sandwich but is yanked away by Vinny.

                    VINNY
        Move it, come on, move it.

He stops outside a shop. We see from the three golden balls
that it's a pawnbroker's. Vinny and dog enter the pawnshop.

INT. PAWNBROKER'S – DAY

Meet Sol who's behind the counter, Vinny's partner in the
pawnshop. He's concentrating on the deal at hand with Bad
Boy Lincoln and has a stone-inspecting monocle to his eye.

                    VINNY
        Bad Boy. Sol.

They are in deep discussion and only Lincoln responds.

                BAD BOY LINCOLN
        Easy.

                    SOL
        Nah, it's a 'moissanite'.

                BAD BOY LINCOLN
        A whatinnite?

                    SOL
        A moissanite is an artificial diamond, Lincoln. It's
        Mickey Mouse mate, spurious, not genuine, and it's
        worth fuck all.

Lincoln's face drops.

                    VINNY

Bad Boy, I keep tellin' ya, stick to being a 'gang-star',
leave this game to me and Sol.

              BAD BOY LINCOLN

Laters.

Lincoln leaves the store. Sol looks round properly at Vinny
and can see that he's accompanied by a dog.

                 SOL (cont'd)

What is that, Vince?

                    VINNY

This is a dog, Sol.

                     SOL

You are not bringing that thing in here.

                    VINNY

What's your problem? It's only a fuckin' dog.

                     SOL

Where did you get it?

                    VINNY

The gypos. Here, they threw it in with a load of moody
gold.

Vince throws a leather bag to Sol who catches it.

                VINNY (cont'd)

You know, gypos, Sol they're always throwing dogs in
with deals.

SOL

Well, it better not be dangerous.

Vinny lets the dog off the lead.

SOL

What do you think you're doing now?

VINNY

I want him to get used to the shop, don't I?

Just then the door opens, and the dog runs out of the shop.
Vinny runs after it.

VINNY (cont'd)

Oi, oi, stop the dog! Come back here, oi …

Vinny goes running after it. Boris comes into the shop.

SOL

All right, Boris? Don't worry about the dog.

BORIS

I'm not.

SOL

What can I do for you, Boris?

BORIS

I have a job for you.

SOL

I already have a job.

                         BORIS
     Fifty grand for half a day's work.

                          SOL
     Go on.

                         BORIS
     I want you to hold up a bookie's.

INT. DOUG'S OFFICE – DAY

Doug the Head and Franky Four Fingers are doing a deal.
Doug has a case open and is admiring a some stones.

                         DOUG
     Ahh. From Russia with love, eh?

Pause. Franky's in a rush.

                 FRANKY FOUR FINGERS
     I have stones to sell, fat to chew and many different
     men to see about many different dogs. So if I am not
     rushing you –

                         DOUG
     Slow down Franky, my son when in Rome –

                 FRANKY FOUR FINGERS
     I am not in Rome, Doug, I am in a rush. Got to make
     the bookie's.

                  DOUG (turns around)
     Bookies? What are you betting on?

                    FRANKY FOUR FINGERS
          Bomber Harris.

                          DOUG
          Oh, the unlicensed boxer, eh? Do you know something
          that I don't?

                    FRANKY FOUR FINGERS
          Bubbi, I probably know a lot you don't.

Doug laughs.

EXT. LONDON STREET – DAY

Sol and Vinny meet up with Tyrone, a very big, fat black
guy. The dog is back with them and they walk to a car.

                          SOL
          He's bad to the bone. Ain'tcha Tyrone?

                        TYRONE
          Course I am.

                          SOL
          Tyrone's going to be driving us. He's done a rally
          driving course, ain'tcha Tyrone?

                        TYRONE
          Course I have.

INT. TYRONE'S CAR – DAY

CUT TO: Sol, Vinny, Tyrone and the dog seated in the car.
Tyrone looks at the dog. The car moves off.

TYRONE

I don't want that dog dribbling on my seats.

VINNY

Your seats? Tyrone, this is a stolen car, mate.

TYRONE

While I'm at the wheel, it's my car. So stop that dog
dribbling on my seats, all right?

Gesturing at the dog.

SOL

I can't believe you found him. Where did it go?

VINNY

It went straight back to the gypos.

SOL

Oh shut up. How could it find them?

VINNY

Well, I don't know, I'm not a dog, Sol. Ask him. It's like
he's a fuckin' homing beacon or something.

EXT. PETROL STATION – DAY

Tyrone pulls into a petrol station braking sharply.

VINNY (cont'd)

Steady on the brakes! Fuck me, I thought you said he
could drive, Sol?

TYRONE

Listen don't you worry about me, jus' worry 'bout that
dog 'pon my seats? All right?

Tyrone gets out. It takes a long time. Once he's safely out,
Vinny leans forward.

VINNY

Oi?

SOL

What?

VINNY

I thought you said he was a getaway driver. What the
fuck can he get away from, eh?

SOL

Don't worry about Tyrone, he can move when he has
to. Just worry about getting us a gun.

VINNY

Yeah?

Vinny pulls out a ridiculously powerful SHOTGUN.

SOL

What's that?

VINNY

This is a shotgun, Sol.

SOL

It's a fuckin' anti-aircraft gun, Vincent.

VINNY
Yeah, well, I wanna raise some pulses don't I?

SOL
You'll raise hell, never mind pulses!

EXT. STREET OUTSIDE BOOKIE'S/
INT. FRANKY'S VAN

Franky Four Fingers gets out of his van. He takes a quick look around and enters the back of his van. There he looks at his suits hanging up.

INT. TYRONE'S CAR OUTSIDE BOOKIES – DAY

The three black guys pull up in Tyrone's car outside the BOOKIE'S. Tyrone stops the car.

TYRONE
That does not look like a bookie's.

VINNY
What have we stopped here for? What's the matter with that space over there?

TYRONE
It's too tight.

VINNY
Too tight? You could land a jumbo fuckin' jet in there.

SOL
Oi, leave him alone, he's a natural, inn't you Tyrone?

TYRONE

'Course I am.

Tyrone starts to accelerate and reverses into the *rear* of the
VAN behind them (i.e. it's parked back-to-back with them).
There's a nasty crash and noise.

EXT. STREET OUTSIDE BOOKIE'S/
INT. FRANKY'S VAN

INT. VAN. Franky is just refastening the case on his arm.
When his van is hit from behind it knocks him out cold.

CUT BACK TO: INT. TYRONE'S CAR.

The three are recovering from the impact of Tyrone hitting
the van. The dog whines.

VINNY

A natural fuckin' idiot! Tyrone, what you done?

SOL

Yeah, Tyrone, what have you done?

TYRONE

Look, you hassle me, you see what happens.

VINNY (to the whining dog)

It's all right, it's all right.

Tyrone makes to move the car forward again.

VINNY

No, don't move it now, otherwise people'll see the

damage. What d'you do that for?

TYRONE

I didn't see it there.

VINNY

It's a four ton truck, Tyrone. It's not as though it's a
packet of fuckin' peanuts is it?

TYRONE

It was at a funny angle.

Vinny and Sol turn to look behind them. They are confused.

VINNY

It's behind you, Tyrone. Whenever you reverse, things
come from behind ya.

The dog starts whining and grabs the back of Sol.

TYRONE

Control that dog as well. Get that dog off him.

SOL

Get that dog off me.

The dog barks.

VINNY

Give that squeaky toy. It shut him up last time.

Sol holds out a palstic squeaky pig ball that was in the
front. The dog grabs it.

> VINNY (to the dog)
> Oi, don't snatch.

The dog swallows the pig in one gulp. The brothers look on in shock.

> SOL
> He can't swallow a whole ball.

Vinny looks bemused. The dog looks up, having completed the task. It barks and this time there's a loud squeak.

INT. AMUSEMENT ARCADE/OFFICE – MORNING

Tommy and Turkish walk from their arcade to the back office. Turkish is holding a pint of milk.

> TURKISH
> Why the fuck did you put Gorgeous George into a bare-knuckle boxing match two days before he had to fight the Bomber?

> TOMMY
> He was half his size. I didn't expect him to get hurt.

> TURKISH
> You put the man into a bare-knuckle boxing match...

He raises his voice.

> TURKISH (cont'd)
> ...What the fuck did you expect? A grease down and a shiatsu?

TOMMY
Who took the jam out of your doughnut?

TURKISH
You took the fuckin' jam out of my doughnut Tommy, you did.

TOMMY
You said get a good deal...

TURKISH
I fail to recognise the correlation between losing 10 grand, hospitalizing Gorgeous, and a good deal?

Pause. There is no correlation as Tommy knows.

TURKISH (cont'd)
How we going to explain this to Brick Top, that his fight isn't going to happen?

TOMMY
We replace the fighter.

TURKISH
Oh, and hope he doesn't notice? And who the fuck are we going to replace him with?

TOMMY
What about John 'The Gun?' Or 'Mad Fist' Willy?

Cut to a shot of 'John the Gun' punching a bag.

Cut to a shot of 'Mad Fist' pulling weights.

TURKISH
You're not exactly Mr Current Affairs, are you
Tommy? 'Mad Fist' went mad ...

INSERT A

Cut to a shot of both 'Mad Fist' going mad...

TURKISH (cont'd)
...and 'The Gun' shot himself.

INSERT B

...and 'The Gun' shooting himself. CUT BACK.

Pause for thought...then Turkish has the look of a man who
has come across a really bright idea.

TURKISH (cont'd)
Jesus!

TOMMY
What?

TURKISH
Let's use the fuckin' pikey.

INT. MICKEY'S CARAVAN – DAY

Mickey, Tommy and Turkish are in mid discussion with the
usual dodgy entourage.

MICKEY
How much you gonna pay us?

TOMMY

Ten k.

MICKEY

Ah me bollocks. Lose more than that running for the
bus.

Mickey and the guys huddle in for a discussion.

MICKEY

All right. I'll do it for a caravan.

TURKISH

A what?

OTHER GYPSIES

A caravan.

MICKEY

Top of the range and all, like.

TOMMY

It was us that wanted a caravan. Anyway what's wrong
with this one?

MICKEY

It's not for me, it's for me mam.

TOMMY

You what?

GYPSY

His mam.

Darren pulls out a photograph of Mickey's mum. It's passed down the line to Tommy and Turkish. A close-up of Mum O'Neil smiling.

INT. BACK OF BRICK TOP'S PUB – DAY

Turkish and Tommy follow Errol through a maze of dark and dingy corridors.

> TURKISH (V/O)
> Brick Top runs an illegal bookie's; they take bets on anything that involves blood and pain. Now I'm changing fighters, Brick Top's gonna exploit the situation.

The mood is sinister – they reach another door, they open up and we are introduced to the aftermath of a dog fight. A circle of blunt faces are exchanging money with one another. A few faces turn round to examine Tommy and Turkish, they frown slightly but carry on about their business once they see they are accompanied by the muscle.

> TURKISH (V/O cont'd)
> He's gonna pull my pants down, grease me up and aim for penetration and if I didn't have the replacement pikey he'd wanna split me in half.

Two dogs are in the ring. One is alive, another covered in blood too but it is dead.
Errol stops Turkish and Tommy and goes over to Brick Top.

> TURKISH (to Tommy)
> They can charm the paint off walls, these fellas.

There is a cage next to Brick Top which has a pit bull terrier in, and Brick Top, who is carrying a cane, pokes it through the cage doors. The dog snarls back. Brick Top notices Turkish and Tommy and motions for them to come over.

                    BRICK TOP
        Look mean now you hairy fucker, won't ya?

He looks at the appalled faces of Turkish and Tommy.

                    BRICK TOP (cont'd)
        Shits himself when you put him in a ring, but poke it
        with a stick and watch his bollocks grow… D'you like
        a dog fight, Turkish?

                    TURKISH
        We've lost Gorgeous George.

                    BRICK TOP
        Sssh.

Brick Top indicates that he would like the noise around him to drop. A tangible silence between the men reflects Brick Top's authority.

                    BRICK TOP
        You're gonna have to repeat that.

                    TURKISH
        We've lost Gorgeous George.

                    BRICK TOP (cont'd)
        Well, where did you lose him? He ain't a set of fuckin'
        car keys is he? And it's not as though he's fuckin'

inconfuckinspicuous now is it?

TURKISH

We're not backing out.

BRICK TOP

You can bet your bollocks to a barn dance you're not backing out.

TOMMY

We're changing the fighter.

Brick Top wasn't expecting anything out of Tommy.

BRICK TOP

Oh fuck me, your lady friend got a voice? And who might you be changing him to, sweetheart?

TURKISH

You won't know him, but he's mustard.

Pause: a look of 'you're kidding' comes over Brick Top's face.

BRICK TOP

Mustard? I don't care if he's Mohammed 'I'm hard Bruce Lee'. You can't change fighters.

TURKISH

Look, you've still got your fight.

BRICK TOP

No, I lose all bets at the bookie's. You can't change fighters at the last minute, so no, I don't have my fight do I, you fuckin' prat?!

TOMMY
You can take bets at the fight.

BRICK TOP
Put a lead on her Turkish, before she gets bitten. And
you don't want to get bitten now do you sweetheart?

Brick Top pauses and gestures to Turkish to come closer and
whispers in his ear.

BRICK TOP (cont'd)
Make sure your man goes down in the fourth. You
understand me now, don't you Turkish?

TURKISH (V/O)
This is the one place I didn't want to be – in his debt,
which now means I'm in his pocket.

BRICK TOP
You're on thin fuckin' ice, my pedigree chums and I
shall be under it when it breaks. Now fuck off.

Brick Top pokes the dog again – more snarling.

INT. NEW YORK STREET OFFICE

INT. LONDON JEWELLERY SHOW
SPLITSCREEN – DAY

Avi is on the phone to Doug – CU's of their respective feet.
Avi in cream socks, Doug in Union Jack socks.

AVI
Doug, where's Franky Four Fingers?

DOUG

I don't know Avi, I'm not his mother. But I'm seeing
him later.

AVI

When later?

DOUG
(The camera pulls back as he stands)
Well, he said he wanted cash so he's coming back after
he's been to a fight.

The camera pulls back from Avi's feet to a wide. The camera
crashes into a serious expression of alarm on Avi's face.

AVI

A fight, what do you mean, what do you mean, a fight?
A boxing match? Is there gambling involved?

DOUG

It's a boxing match Avi, a boxing match.

Avi isn't happy.

AVI

Did he have a case with him?

DOUG

Yes, he had a case.

AVI

And this schmuck is gambling? You're talking about
Franky 'I've got a problem with gambling' fuckin' Four
Fingers, Doug.

                    DOUG

    Avi, I'm not telepathic!

                     AVI

    Well you're plenty fuckin' stupid, I'll give you that!
    You have any idea why they call him Franky Four
    Fingers, Doug?

                    DOUG

    No, I have no idea.
                     AVI

    Well, because he makes stupid bets with dangerous
    people, and when he doesn't pay up, they give him the
    chop, Doug, and I'm not talking about his fuckin'
    foreskin either!

                    DOUG

    Avi, I'm sure he can pay.

Avi pulls a face like 'what kind of a stupid question is that?'.

                     AVI

    Well, not with my goods he isn't.

He then turns his attention to Rosebud.

                 AVI (cont'd)

    You got a tooth brush? We're going to London. D'you
    hear that, (shouting) Doug? I'm coming to London!

CUT TO: The phone is slammed down by Avi.
CUT TO: American cab door being slammed.
CUT TO: Avi taking pills and drinking water slamming
           cup down on airplane table.

CUT TO: Concorde taking off.
CUT TO: Passport being stamped in UK.
CUT TO: Black cab light going off.

INT. DOUG'S OFFICE – DAY

                    DOUG (welcoming)
        Avi!

Avi is now standing in front of Doug with Rosebud in tow.

                    AVI
        Shut up and sit down you big, bald fuck.

Pause.

                    AVI (cont'd)
        I don't like leaving my own country, Doug, and I
        especially don't like leaving it for anything less than
        warm sandy beaches, and cocktails with little straw hats.

                    DOUG
        Well, we've got sandy beaches.

                    AVI
        So who the fuck wants to see 'em? I hope that you can
        appreciate the concern I have for my friend, Franky.

Pause.

                    AVI (cont'd)
        I'm gonna find him Doug, and you're going to help me
        find him, and we're gonna start at that fight.

INT. TYRONE'S CAR OUTSIDE BOOKIE'S – NIGHT

The three black guys are still sitting in the car, waiting for a sighting of Franky. The occasional squeak comes from the dog. Sol is eating crisps.

> VINNY
> How am I going to get it out?

> SOL
> It'll probably cough it up.

> VINNY
> Do you think he'll be all right?

Sol shrugs.

> SOL
> I hope not.

> VINNY
> Look, are we gonna rob this bookie's or what?

> SOL
> Yes, big man.

> TYRONE
> What are we waiting for anyway?

> SOL
> We are waiting for a man with four fingers, carrying a briefcase, Tyrone.

TYRONE

And why's that?

SOL

Because the deal is the Russian gets the case, we get the money.

Sol munches on crisps.

TYRONE

What's in the case?

VINNY

Oh for fuck's sake Tyrone. Just concentrate on the steering wheel.

EXT. CAESAR'S PALACE, STREATHAM – NIGHT

Doug and Avi come around a dimly lit corner, slap into a doorman.

AVI

Jesus.

DOORMAN 1

Private night tonight chaps.

DOUG

Yes, I'm well aware of that my son. That's why we're here.

Doug passes him TICKETS. The doorman steps to the side and they go down an alleyway.

                              DOUG
Well done. This is the back way in.

                              AVI
Oh really? I thought it was the front.

They come to another doorman.

                           DOORMAN 2
Private night tonight chaps.

                              AVI
We know that. That's exactly why we're here.

INT. CAESAR'S PALACE, STREATHAM – NIGHT

Avi and Doug come into a red plush interior and find yet
another DOORMAN.

                           DOORMAN 3
Tickets.

                              AVI
Are we ever going to get into this place? Huh?

                              DOUG
Avi, Avi, you gotta understand. This ain't exactly
Vegas, and this ain't exactly legal.

                              AVI
I'm not looking for Vegas and I'm not looking for
legal, I'm looking for Franky fuckin' Four Fingers.

DOUG
I know that, and he said that, er, he said he's gonna be here.

AVI
Well, if there's gambling involved, he'll be here.

CUT TO: BRICK TOP.

A heavy looking guy, JACK THE ALL SEEING EYE, is talking to Brick Top along with his colleague SALT PETER. Jack and Peter are obviously serious characters in order to warrant attention from Brick Top.

JACK THE ALL SEEING EYE
Let's not have a fuck-up. You're not gonna let us down now, are ya?

BRICK TOP
He's going down in the fourth. Don't you worry about that Peter.

Brick Top nods to Peter too as he walks off.

INT. TYRONE'S CAR OUTSIDE BOOKIE'S – NIGHT – CONTINUOUS

Sol turns round just as a man is stepping into the bookies: he is carrying a case.

SOL (cont'd)
Ooh, was that him?

VINNY
I don't know. How many fingers did he have?

SOL
I'm sorry, I couldn't get the 'by-noculars' out in time.

VINNY
Well look, let's not stand on ceremony, mate, let's start the show.

Sol and Vinny get out of the car and go up to the bookie's, leaving Tyrone in the car. There's a glass door. Sol pushes it open, and Vinny walks in first, while Sol hangs back with the shotgun.

INT. BOOKIE'S – NIGHT

As they come in they now have balaclavas on. Vinny doesn't mince around and goes straight to the counter, where the head clerk, Pauline, is on the phone. Vinny points a gun at her.

PAULINE
Do you know who this bookie's belongs to?

VINNY
Look if you know what's good for you, right, you'll give me everything you've got.

He is cut short, as Pauline triggers a button under the counter and a SECURITY SCREEN comes flying up at a very rapid rate of knots, protecting all the counters. This has the unfortunate consequence of taking Vinny with it. Poor Vin is shot straight to the ceiling, all we can see is half a body and his desperately-searching-for-ground-legs.

Needless to say this leaves Sol in a bit of a bewildered state. He's looking the wrong way at the critical moment and is left wondering what happened, not having seen Vince caught at the top of the screen. Sol extracts the enormous SHOTGUN. He spins round looking for his colleague. A muffled noise tells him to look up. We see this on CCTV.

SOL (cont'd)
Vince, Vince, what you doing up there, Vince?

A few groans emanate from the other side of the screen.

VINNY
What does it look it like I'm doing up here?

Sol panics some more, and decides that emergency action is called for. Sol raises the gun and fires into the side of the wall. There's an enormous explosion and a clear hole is made in the side of the wall. The powerful kick from the gun also makes Sol momentarily airborne.

VINNY (off camera)
This is starting to hurt, Solomon!

Sol pulls himself together and marches up to the hole in the wall that the shot created and pokes the gun through.

SOL
Drop the screen now!

The screen comes down with a thud. Vince comes down with just as serious a thud. He lets out another groan.

SOL

How you doing, Vince?

A weakened voice retorts.

VINNY

I'd be doing a lot better if you'd stop using my name.

Consoled that his colleague is not dead, it's back to business for Sol. He raises the gun and pulls his fiercest face.

SOL

Fill that bag.

PAULINE

All bets are off.

SOL

I am not in here to make a fuckin' bet!

PAULINE (pointing)

Appreciated but all bets are off! If all bets are off, then there can't be any money, can there?

There is a pause. Sol knows he's fucked. She points to a blackboard that clearly states 'ALL BETS ARE OFF'.

SOL

I ain't fuckin' buying that.

PAULINE

Well that's handy because I ain't fuckin' selling it, it's a fact!

104

Pause.

> SOL

What have you got?

> PAULINE

Nothing really. A few coins but no notes.

Sol's temper does have a limit. He shoots up at the ceiling, debris falls. Some debris falls on Vinny still sprawled on the floor. Sol points at the man on the floor who is carrying the case.

> SOL (cont'd)

Show me your hands.

The man holds his hands up. He has got a perfect set of five fingers on both hands.

> SOL (cont'd)

You've got five fingers. God!

CUT TO: Sol is at the counter with the bag of coins. Sol picks them up and frowns, he's not happy with a bag full of change. (He has to put his gun down to rifle through the bag.)

> SOL (cont'd)

Copper coins? What do you mean copper fuckin' coins?

Pauline sees her opportunity and grabs the shotgun. Sol goes for it too, but he's beaten to it. Sol ducks, pulling Vince with him, Pauline lets out a shot in their direction. The security screen comes flying back up. Sol grabs the bag of copper coins, grabs Vince and marches towards the door.

EXT. GLASS DOORS OF BOOKIE'S – NIGHT

They push the door: nothing happens. There is no going back. Sol starts to kick the glass door, but it doesn't budge.

> VINNY
>
> It won't open because it's a security door.

With panic rising swiftly, Sol doesn't fuck around. He hands the bag of coins to Vinny.

> SOL
>
> Hold that.

He takes aim with the handgun and fires. The bullet shatters the glass but it doesn't break through. The bullet ricochets off the glass door. He fires again. The bullet tears through the bag of coins, which empties its contents at Vinny's and Sol's feet, and seems to hit poor Vinny in the thigh.

> SOL
>
> Fuck!

> VINNY
>
> My leg!

Sol sinks to the floor, he has given up. He checks Vinny's leg.

> SOL
>
> What are you moaning about? It didn't even touch ya.

They pull off their balaclavas. Cut to a shot of them on CCTV. They look up and see the camera.

> VINNY
>
> We're fucked.

At that point Tyrone appears and pushes the door open. The door was open the whole time – only Sol was pushing it the wrong way.

> TYRONE
>
> What the fuck are you two doing?

Sol and Vinny scramble up and dash out of the door.

INT FRANKY'S VAN/EXT STREET OUTSIDE BOOKIE'S

Franky begins to wake up.

EXT. BOOKIE'S – NIGHT

They stumble out into the street and into the car.

> VINNY
>
> Get us outta here, Tyrone.

Tyrone pulls out.

Franky Four Fingers stands up and appears from the back of his van. He was locked in due to the fact that Tyrone's car was blocking his exit.

EXT. BOOKIE'S – NIGHT

Tyrone takes an interest in the man from the van (i.e. Franky) seeing that he's carrying a case and the case is connected to his wrist.

                    SOL
Tyrone, what are you doing?

                  SOL/VINNY
Get us outta here!

EXT. STREET OUTSIDE BOOKIE'S/ INT. TYRONE'S
CAR – NIGHT

Franky is locking his van when Tyrone hits him over the
head. Franky falls to the ground. Tyrone tries to take the
case off him but it's handcuffed to his wrist. So he has little
choice but to pick him up and throw him into the back of
the car with Vinny and Sol. The dog whimpers.

                   VINNY
Who the fuck is this man, Tyrone?

                  TYRONE
He's a man with four fingers and a briefcase, Vinny.

INT. BOXING RING – NIGHT

In one corner is Mickey, Tommy and Turkish with him.
There's a big crowd waiting for this.

              MASTER OF CEREMONIES
In the red corner we have the young and unchallenged,
cut-throat of calamity, meaner than Beelzebub's
conscience cleaner...

CUT TO TURKISH AND MICKEY

TURKISH
So, Mickey, you're going down in the fourth. Is that
clear?

MICKEY
Just make sure he doesn't kill me before the fuckin'
fourth.

MASTER OF CEREMONIES (cont'd)
…So give it up for the bone-crunching, one-punch
machine gun, Mickey!

A murky sound of displeasure emanates from the audience
around the arena. They don't know who he is and don't care
either.

MASTER OF CEREMONIES (cont'd)
And in the other corner, a man …

CUT TO: TURKISH AND MICKEY

TURKISH
Now, I know he looks like a fat fucker. Well, he is a fat
fucker, but he's dirty and he's dangerous.

MASTER OF CEREMONIES (cont'd)
…Bomber 'The Mad Man' Harris!

The audience goes mad. It's hard to tell whether it's out of
affectionate enthusiasm or just enthusiasm. Bomber struts
around the ring.

CUT BACK TO: TURKISH AND MICKEY

Turkish takes off Mickey's hat and removes his cigarette from his mouth.

TURKISH

Now try and look like a fighter.

MASTER OF CEREMONIES (cont'd)

...Let's...get ready to rrrrrummmmmble.

The two come out to fight and touch gloves. As the bell goes Bomber Harris head-butts Mickey who reels back, dazed. They pace each other for a second. Then Mickey lets one go. It hits Bomber Harris square on the jaw. He hits the floor – he's positively out cold. We crashtrack into various characters' reactions: Brick Top, Jack the All Seeing Eye, Salt Peter, Turkish and Tommy, etc. All are in shock. Mickey is a bit embarrassed and wanders around the ring.
It's all over. Brick Top storms out but is stopped by Jack and Salt Peter who are obviously not happy.

JACK THE ALL SEEING EYE

Do you realise I've just done fuckin' forty grand down you? What's the fuckin' crack?

Brick Top is obviously annoyed but uses restraint.

BRICK TOP

I'll make it up to ya.

SALT PETER

Well I ain't fucking happy, Brick Top.

BRICK TOP

I'll make it up to ya. I promise. Stand on me.

Brick Top walks on a couple of paces.

> BRICK TOP (cont'd)
> Ohh, that fuckin' pikey's put me in it.

Another character, NEIL, approaches Brick Top.

> NEIL
> Well thanks for the tip, Brick Top –

Brick Top grabs Neil by the face – to the surprise of both
Brick Tops boy's and Neil.

> BRICK TOP
> Listen you fuckin' fringe. If I throw a dog a bone, I
> don't want to know if it tastes good or not. You stop
> me again whilst I'm walking and I'll cut your fuckin'
> jacobs off.

Brick Top sticks a knife in Neil, who crumples. Brick Top
walks away and Neil raises his hand to see it blood soaked.

EXT. PAWNBROKER'S – NIGHT

Boris is admiring the outside of the shop. He walks in.

INT. PAWNBROKER'S – NIGHT

Franky is tied up on a stool in the back room. There is a tea
cosy on his head. The black guys are standing around.

> VINNY
> He's here

SOL

Well, you explain it to him.

Boris waves the black guys to come into the corridor *so they can talk without being heard.*

BORIS

What you doing with him?

SOL

The case was attached to his arm.

BORIS

So why didn't you chop it off?

Sol looks horrified at the thought.

SOL

Why?

VINNY

We ain't fuckin' butchers, Boris.

BORIS

But he has the case?

VINNY

Look, we, well, you have, a problem.

BORIS

What?

SOL

There weren't much cash at the bookie's

                              BORIS
    Ah. OK.

Boris pulls out ten thousand pounds in a huge wad and
holds it out to Sol.

                              BORIS
    Here's the ten grand.

                               SOL
    Nah.

                              VINNY
    Nah. Keep it. We want this, well at least half of this.

Vinny holds up the stone: the atmosphere changes. Boris
looks slightly cross.

                              BORIS
    What was in the case was mine. What was in the
    bookie's was yours. OK, well, there wasn't much but
    here's the ten large to help the situation.

                              VINNY
    Nah, I'm afraid it's too late for that. We want half of
    this and that's because we're being generous.

Vinny is becoming frustrated and raises his voice.

                          VINNY (cont'd)
    I mean we could by all rights keep the whole fuckin'
    stone, *Boris*.

He holds up the diamond. Boris's eyes follow him as he and
Sol walk back into the room where Franky is. Vinny puts the
diamond back into the case and shuts it. Boris grimaces, puts
in his ear plug, pulls out a gun from God knows where, and
within a second shoots poor Franky in the face. Franky's body
disappears off the stool that he was sitting on. The black guys
are stunned into silence. Boris walks into the room.

> BORIS
> Drop the gun fat boy. You fuckin' idiots. He could not
> know my name. Give me the stone.

The black guys are left with their mouths open, everything
just changed gear and they weren't expecting that.

> VINNY
> It's in the case.

> BORIS
> What?

Boris has to remove an ear plug.

> VINNY
> It's in the case.

> BORIS
> You put the stone in the case. Then open the case and
> give me the stone.

The pause continues.

> SOL
> The only man who knew the combination, you just shot.

Boris appears a little bothered by this. He puts his gun away mumbling some obscenity in Russian and whips out a machete that he was concealing about his person. He pulls the case towards him and brings the machete down with full force. We can tell by the black guys' reactions that it was some part of Franky's anatomy.

INT. AMUSEMENT ARCADE/BACK OFFICE – DAY

Turkish walks down the corridor from the arcade into his office. He is wary. As he walks into his office, has a quick look around and makes his way to the safe behind the painting on the wall, the voice-over begins.

> TURKISH (V/O)
> Now it's not too clever to hang about after Mickey's performance. Brick Top in short will be looking to kill Tommy, Mickey and myself. I know he's looking for us but I don't have a choice.

He decides to put the kettle on. We see that the kettle is already boiled.

> TURKISH (V/O cont'd)
> I'm happy to leave the country but I need money to do so, but any money I have is in the safe which is in the office. Once I have that it's –

> ERROL (interrupting)
> Oink, oink.

Turkish jumps and drops the sugar bowl. Errol and John are sitting on the other side of the office.

                    TURKISH
Shit.

                    ERROL
So that's where you keep the sugar.

                    TURKISH
What brings you two here, run out of pants to sniff?

                    ERROL
That sounds like hostility, doesn't it, John?

                    JOHN
And we don't like hostility, do we, Errol?

                    ERROL
No, we don't, John.

Errol and John rise and walk towards Turkish, who steps
backwards into Brick Top. Brick Top looks down at his shoes.

                    BRICK TOP
Eh. I just had them polished.

Pause.

                    BRICK TOP (cont'd)
Go and put the kettle on.

Turkish adapts to his new circumstances.

                    TURKISH
You take sugar?

                        118

> **BRICK TOP**
> No thank you, Turkish, I'm sweet enough.

INT. PAWN BROKER'S – NIGHT (cont'd)

We are still in the backroom with the brothers and Boris.
Boris wraps up the severed arm in newspaper and picks up
the case. Pointing to the ground:

> **BORIS**
> He's now your problem.OK? You can keep the ten
> grand along with the body, but if I see you again…

Boris gestures threateningly, the brothers back away even
further.

> **BORIS**
> …you motherfuckers. Well, look at him.

> He points to Franky. He then walks out of the
> pawnshop casual as you like.

INT. AMUSEMENT ARCADE/BACK OFFICE – DAY

Brick Top is now sitting down.

> **BRICK TOP**
> I've got a bare-knuckle fight in a couple of days. I want
> to use the pikey.

> **TURKISH**
> All right, of course.

                    BRICK TOP
    Of course, fuckin', of course, I wasn't asking I was
    telling.

His voice drops and he speaks slowly and seriously.

                    BRICK TOP (cont'd)
    But this time I do want him to go down in the fourth.
    And I do mean it this time.

He stands and walks to the painting and pushes it to the
side, revealing the safe.

                    BRICK TOP (cont'd)
    Now I know you come back here to open your safe. So
    now you can open it.

There is nothing Turkish can do.

INT. AMUSEMENT ARCADE – CONTINUOUS

Brick Top exits the back office with Errol and John. He's
holding the contents of Turkish's safe.

                    BRICK TOP
    He's been a busy little bastard that Turkish.

                    ERROL
    I think you've let him get away with enough all ready,
    guvner.

Brick Top looks round with some concern.

BRICK TOP
It can get you into a lot of trouble thinking, Errol, I
shouldn't do so much of it.

Pause.

BRICK TOP (cont'd)
Right, that takes care of one little piggy, now find me
the silly sods who blagged the bookie's. Find 'em today.

EXT. CARAVAN CAMPSITE – DAY

Turkish and Tommy walk through the campsite. Mickey's
Mum is sitting in her chair outside the caravan. Tommy has
produced a bunch of flowers from somewhere. Turkish finds
this a great surprise. Mrs O'Neil is wary.

TOMMY
Top of the morning to you, Mrs O'Neil.

MUM O'NEIL
Tommy.

TURKISH
You're a snake in the grass, ain't you, Tommy? Where
did they come from?

MUM O'NEIL
You're looking for my boy, are ya?

TURKISH
Do you know where I can find him Mrs O'Neil?

                    MUM O'NEIL
     Yeah.

Pause.

                    TURKISH
     I don't suppose you would you like to share that
     information with me, would ya?

                    MUM O'NEIL
     I don't want you getting my boy into any trouble,
     d'you hear me? He's my only boy, and he's a good boy.

Pause.

                MUM O'NEIL (cont'd)
     He's coursing.

EXT. GYPSY CAMPSITE/INT. CAR/EXT. COUNTRY
LANE – DAY

EXT. GYPSY CAMPSITE – DAY – CONTINUOUS

Turkish and Tommy walk away from Mrs O'Neil.

                    TOMMY
     What's coursing?

                    TURKISH
     Hare coursing.

INT. CAR – DAY CONTINUOUS

Turkish and Tommy drive to the hare coursing field.

                         124

TURKISH (cont'd)
They set two lurchers – they're dogs before you ask…

EXT. COUNTRY FIELD – DAY – CONTINUOUS

They are now walking through a field.

TURKISH (cont'd)
…on a hare. And the hare has to outrun the dogs.

TOMMY
So, what if it doesn't?

TURKISH
Well, the big rabbit gets fucked, doesn't it?

Tommy looks a bit taken aback by this statement. He stops
and stops Turkish.

TOMMY
Proper fucked?

TURKISH
Yeah, Tommy. Before 'zee Germans' get there.

They carry on walking.

INT. BRICK TOP'S

CUT TO: CU MONITOR OF SOL AND VINNY IN THE
BOOKIE'S, UNMASKED AND SLUMPED AGAINST
THE WALL.

                    BRICK TOP (off camera)
            Do you know these tits, Errol?

                         ERROL
            I know a lot of tits, governor but I don't know any as
            quite fuckin' stupid as these two.

                       BRICK TOP
            John?

                         JOHN
            I can't help, guv.

            Monitor shows Tyrone coming through the door.

                         ERROL
            Ah, Tyrone…

                      ERROL/JOHN
            You silly fat bastard.

            EXT. HARE COURSING FIELD – DAY

            Turkish and Tommy have found Mickey who is in the middle
            of a field and is betting with various other dodgy characters.

                        TURKISH
            Well, do you want to do it?

                        MICKEY
            That depends.

                        TURKISH
            On what?

MICKEY

On you buying this caravan.

Darren proffers a CATALOGUE on fancy caravans and
Mickey points to the picture of the Rolls Royce of caravans.

MICKEY

Ah, not the rouge, the rose.

TURKISH

That's not the same caravan.

MICKEY

That's not the same fight.

TURKISH

It's twice the fuckin' size of the last one.

MICKEY

Turkish, the fight is twice the size. And my mam still
needs a caravan. And I like to look after me mam. It's a
fair deal, take it!

TURKISH

Mickey, you're lucky we aren't worm food after your
last performance. Buying a tart's mobile palace is a
little fuckin' rich.

There is a pause while Mickey and the other gypsies start to
frown as Turkish's words sink in. Turkish looks a little sheepish.

TURKISH (cont'd)

I wasn't calling your mum a tart. I just meant –

Everyone relaxes.

                    MICKEY
          Ah, save your breath for cooling your porridge. So
          now look …

He goes into high speed description that neither Turkish or
we have a clue what he's saying.

                    MICKEY (cont'd)
          … She's terribly partial to the periwinkle blue. Have I
          made myself clear, boys?

                    TURKISH
          Yeah, that's perfectly clear Mickey. Just give me one
          minute to confer with my colleague.

Turkish and Tommy step to one side while Mickey and the
pikeys confer too.

                    TURKISH
          Did you understand one single word of what he just
          said?

The gypsies interrupt.

                    MICKEY
          I'll tell you what I'm going to do.

Pause.

                    MICKEY (cont'd)
          I'll bet you for it.

TURKISH

You'll what?

GYPSIES

He'll bet ya for it.

TURKISH

What, like Tommy did last time? Do me a favour.

MICKEY

I'll do you a favour, you have first bet. If I win I get the
caravan and the boys get a pair of them shoes.

CUT TO: Close-up of Turkish and Tommy's feet in plastic
bags.

MICKEY

If I lose…oh fuck it, I'll do the fight for free.

Turkish considers this, uneasily. He looks at the dogs. They
look keen and fit.

TURKISH (V/O)

Now the last thing I really want to do is to bet a pikey.
However, I don't really have much of a choice.
Somehow I've got to get him to fight. If I lose, well, I
don't even want to think about losing.

TURKISH

OK, I reckon the hare gets fucked.

MICKEY

What proper fucked?

The gypsies laugh. So does Tommy until he looks at Turkish. Mickey and the pikeys set off to start the race.

The next part will be a montage of the hare coursing, the pikeys and Tyrone being hunted by Errol and John.

EXT. NEWSAGENTS – DAY

Tyrone leaves the shop reading a newspaper.

INT. ERROL'S CAR – DAY

Slow motion. Errol and John are looking for Tyrone.

EXT. HARE COURSING FIELD – DAY

Slow motion. Cut back to the dogs. C/U of the pikeys and their fingers skilfully dealing in money.

EXT. NEWSAGENT'S – DAY

Tyrone looks around, sensing danger.

INT. ERROL'S CAR – DAY

Slow motion. Errol and John are still looking.

EXT. HARE COURSING FIELD – DAY

Slow motion. The dogs are frisky. More money changes hands. Mickey smokes.

INT. ERROL'S CAR – DAY

Slow motion. Errol sees Tyrone.

EXT. HARE COURSING FIELD – DAY

Slow motion. The dogs are set loose.

EXT. NEWSAGENT'S – DAY

Slow motion. Tyrone begins to run.

EXT. HARE COURSING FIELD – DAY

Slow motion. The hare sees the dogs and starts to run.

EXT. LONDON STREET – DAY

Slow motion. Tyrone runs around a corner, the car behind him.

INT. ERROL'S CAR – DAY

Slow motion. Errol opens his door.

EXT. HARE COURSING FIELD – DAY

Slow motion. The hare is still running.

INT. ERROL'S CAR – DAY

Slow motion. Errol gets out of the car.

EXT. HARE COURSING FIELD – DAY

Slow motion. The hare is still running, the dogs chasing

EXT. LONDON STREET – DAY

Slow motion. Errol and John begin to bundle Tyrone into the boot of the car.

EXT. HARE COURSING FIELD – DAY

Slow motion. The dogs move out in a pincer movement.

EXT. LONDON STREET – DAY

Slow motion. Errol and John bundle Tyrone into the boot of the car.

EXT. HARE COURSING FIELD – DAY

The dogs move in.

INT. BOOT OF ERROL'S CAR – DAY

Poor Tyrone is bleeding in the boot of a car.

EXT. HARE COURSING FIELD – DAY

Slow motion. The dogs move in closer.

INT. BRICK TOP'S PUB CORRIDOR – DAY

Tyrone is dragged through by Brick Top's henchmen.

EXT. HARE COURSING FIELD – DAY

The dogs move in closer still.

INT. BRICK TOP'S PUB CORRIDOR – DAY

Slow motion. Tyrone struggles to break free.

EXT. HARE COURSING FIELD – DAY

Slow motion. The hare continues to elude the dogs.

INT. BRICK TOP'S PUB CORRIDOR – DAY

Tyrone is led towards the dog fight area.

EXT. HARE COURSING FIELD – DAY

Slow motion. The hare changes direction, dogs follow.

INT. BRICK TOP'S PUB, DOG FIGHT AREA – DAY

Tyrone is thrown into the pit.

EXT. HARE COURSING FIELD – DAY

Slow motion. The dogs are moving in.

INT. BRICK TOP'S PUB, DOG FIGHT AREA – DAY

Brick Top asks questions. Tyrone paces. Brick Top continues
to ask questions. Tyrone isn't playing the game.

EXT. HARE COURSING FIELD – DAY

Slow motion. The dogs are moving in.

INT. BRICK TOP'S PUB, DOG FIGHT AREA – DAY

A rabid Neapolitan mastiff pit bull hybrid that is attached to
the end of a long chain with a lasso at the other end is
brought in. It will quite clearly savage anything in its way. A
man stands on the edge of the pit controlling it.

EXT. HARE COURSING FIELD – DAY

Slow motion. The dogs are moving in.

INT. BRICK TOP'S PUB, DOG FIGHT AREA – DAY

The dogs bark viciously as their chains are loosened.

EXT. HARE COURSING FIELD – DAY

Slow motion. The dogs are moving in.

INT. BRICK TOP'S PUB, DOG FIGHT AREA – DAY

The dog bites Tyrone in the leg.

EXT. HARE COURSING FIELD – DAY

Slow motion. The hare almost gets caught.

INT. BRICK TOP'S PUB, DOG FIGHT AREA – DAY – CONTINUOUS

Tyrone shouts in panic, we come out of slow motion into real time.

> TYRONE
> OK, I'll fuckin' tell you.

EXT. HARE COURSING FIELD – DAY

Slow motion. The dogs get close.

INT. BRICK TOP'S PUB, DOG FIGHT AREA – DAY

> TYRONE
> Get those dogs off me. I'll tell you who robbed your bookie's.

EXT. HARE COURSING FIELD – DAY

The hare escapes the jaws of the dogs and is off. Turkish and Tommy's mouths drop as they watch the hare pull away.

> MICKEY
> (passes brochure to Turkish)
> Periwinkle blue, eh boys.

> TOMMY
> Who's proper fucked now then?

EXT. COUNTRY LANE/INT. CAR – DAY

Turkish is walking back through the fields with Tommy.

TOMMY

There's something very wrong with this, it was us that
wanted to buy a caravan off of him.

TURKISH

Why didn't you 'bus' a cap in his ass' then Tommy?
Mind you, you'd do more damage if you threw it at
him.

TOMMY

You saying I can't shoot?

TURKISH

Oh no, Tommy, I wasn't saying you can't shoot, I
know you can't shoot. What I was saying is that six-
pound piece of shit stuck in your trousers there would
do more damage if you fed it to him.

TOMMY

You saying the gun don't work?

TURKISH

You tried it?

Tommy frowns.

CUT TO: INT. CAR

Tommy sticks the gun out the window, squeezes his eyes
closed and pulls the trigger. Nothing happens.

TURKISH

Whoops.

TOMMY

I want to see that sneaky fuckin' Russian.

INT. PAWNBROKERS – BACK ROOM – DAY

Vin and Sol are trying to solve the problem of Franky's
body. Bad Boy Lincoln has been called in to help.

BAD BOY LINCOLN

What has he got a tea cosy on his head for?

SOL

To keep his head warm.

BAD BOY LINCOLN

What happened to him?

SOL

He got shot in the face, Lincoln. I would have thought
that was obvious.

BAD BOY LINCOLN

What did you do that for? Do you mistake him for a
rabbit? What do you want me to do about it?

VINNY

Sort it out.

BAD BOY LINCOLN

I'm not a fuckin' witch doctor.

SOL

But you are a bad boy Yardie, and bad boy Yardies are
supposed to know how to get rid of bodies.

BAD BOY LINCOLN
I create 'em the bodies. I don't erase the bodies.

EXT. PAWNBROKER'S – DAY – CONTINUOUS

Drill going through a door lock. John opens the door. Errol goes back to the car which is parked down the street. The window slides down.

ERROL
It looks like we're in, guvner.

BRICK TOP
Goodie gum drops. Get us a cup of tea, would you, Errol?

INT. PAWNBROKERS – BACK ROOM – DAY – CONTINUOUS

Vin, Lincoln and Sol are arguing.

SOL
Grab hold of his legs.

BAD BOY LINCOLN
What do you think I'm going to grab him by his fucking ears?

The interconnecting door to the front room of the shop opens slowly.

BRICK TOP
Hope this is not a bad moment.

They drop the body. Bad Boy Lincoln looks alarmed. Sol looks at Vin, Vin looks at Lincoln. The silence continues.

                    BRICK TOP (cont'd)
          Do you know who I am?

                    BAD BOY LINCOLN
          I do.

                    BRICK TOP
          Good. That'll save me some time then.

                    VINNY
          Well I don't.

Brick Top sits down and focuses his attention on the body.

                    BRICK TOP
          You're always gonna have problems lifting a body in
          one piece. Apparently the best thing to do is cut up a
          corpse into six pieces and pile it all together.

                    SOL
          Would somebody mind telling me, who are you?

                    BRICK TOP
          And when you've got your six pieces you gotta get rid
          of 'em, 'cause it's no good leaving it in the deep freeze
          for your mum to discover, now is it?

As he says this, the door opens and in walks Errol. He passes Brick Top a cup of tea in a take-away container.

BRICK TOP (cont'd)
Then I hear the best thing to do is feed them to pigs.
You gotta starve the pigs for a few days, then the sight
of a chopped up body will look like curry to a pisshead.
You gotta shave the heads of your victims and pull the
teeth out, for the sake of the piggies' digestion. You
could do this afterwards of course, but you don't want
to go sieving through pigshit, now do you?

Sol and Bad Boy Lincoln look at each other. Sol's bewildered
and Bad Boy Lincoln is worried.

BRICK TOP (cont'd)
They will go through bone like butter. You need at
least sixteen pigs to finish the job in one sitting, so be
wary of any man who keeps a pig farm. They will go
through a body that weighs two hundred pounds in
about eight minutes – that means that a single pig can
consume two pounds of uncooked flesh every minute...

Pause.

BRICK TOP (cont'd)
Hence the expression: 'as greedy as a pig'.

Brick Top sips his tea. Pause.

VINNY
Well, thank you for that, that's a great weight off my
mind. Now, I mean, if you wouldn't mind telling me
who the fuck you are? Apart from someone who feeds
people to pigs, of course.

Brick Top stands up.

> BRICK TOP
> Do you know what Nemesis means?

There is a pause and they exchange glances.

> BRICK TOP (cont'd)
> A righteous infliction of retribution manifested by an
> appropriate agent, personified in this case by a horrible
> cunt. Me.

Brick Top opens the door, walks across the room and into
the outer office. Then he opens the door into the shop.

> BRICK TOP (cont'd)
> Gentlemen.

We can see that a number of body bags have been laid out on
the floor and the entire shop is now covered in plastic sheeting.
Six very large men with aprons on (including Errol and John)
are standing around wanting to get busy with kebab knives.
Tyrone is with them, all trussed up in a body bag.

INT. HATTON GARDEN PUB – DAY

Doug, Avi, Alex, Susi and Rosebud are in the pub.

> AVI
> Why can't you find me Franky, Doug?

> DOUG
> Avi what do you want me to do? I'm not a bounty hunter.

                              SUSI
            What about Tony? You know Bullet Tooth Tony?
INT. TOPLESS BAR – DAY – FLASHBACK

It is clear from the film stock, the outfits and hairstyles that
we are back in the 80s. Bullet Tooth Tony is entering a
topless bar. Music plays.

INT. HATTON GARDEN PUB – DAY (cont'd)

                               AVI
            Who's Bullet Tooth…?

INT. TOPLESS BAR – DAY – FLASHBACK

Charlie is being expansive and welcoming.

                            CHARLIE
            …Tony!

                             TONY
            You silly fuck.

Cut back to the conversation.

                             DOUG
            He's a liability.

Susi interrupts.

                         SUSI (cont'd)
            He'll find you Moses and the burning bush if you pay
            him to.

                              145

INT. TOPLESS BAR – DAY – FLASHBACK (cont'd)

Charlie is waving a gun. Things have got aggressive.

CHARLIE
You are gonna die, Tony!

INT. HATTON GARDEN PUB – DAY (cont'd)

Back to the conversation.

SUSI
He got shot six times and had all the bullets moulded
into gold.

Charlie opens up, he fires two shots straight into Tony. The
girls are sheltering from the bullets. The music plays on.

CHARLIE
I shoot you! You go down!

ALEX
Yeah, he's got two in his teeth that Dad did for him,
so he loves Dad.

INT. TOPLESS BAR – DAY – FLASHBACK (cont'd)

Charlie fires another three bullets into Tony. He's still upright.

CHARLIE
Why don't you fuckin' die!

INT. HATTON GARDEN PUB – DAY (cont'd)

Conversation continues.

                              ALEX
        He is the best chance you got of finding Franky.

                              AVI
        Six times?

INT. TOPLESS BAR – DAY – FLASHBACK (cont'd)

Charlie shoots Tony again. He buckles against the wall.

INT. PUB – DAY (cont'd)

Conversation continues.

                              DOUG
          In one sitting.

INT. TOPLESS BAR – DAY – FLASHBACK (cont'd)

Tony is standing there with six bullets in him, bleeding all
over the carpet. As he talks blood courses its way out of his
mouth down his front.

                              TONY
        Ohhh, you're in trouble now!

Tony extracts a sword from somewhere. Fear has set into
Charlie's face and rendered him useless.

INT. HATTON GARDEN PUB – DAY (cont'd)

Conversation continues.

AVI

That sounds promising. What are we waiting for?

Doug sighs and looks away.

INT. CAR – DAY

CU of a car phone. It rings. Bullet Tooth Tony is hitting
something with his car door. He pulls a bloodied man up into
shot and throws him out of the way, then reaches for the phone.

TONY

Bonjour?

INT. PAWNBROKER'S – DAY

The black guys are now lying in the body bags. Sol is
making a desperate appeal to Brick Top.

BRICK TOP

What have you got to tell me that's so fucking important?

SOL

Mr Pulford, why do you think we got a dead man
missing an arm in our office?

BRICK TOP

Talk to me, tell me.

SOL

Four days. You give us four days and I'll get you a
stone the size of a fucking home. I kid you not.

Brick Top considers this, and has a look at Errol who is more than enthusiastic to get on with the job at hand.

> BRICK TOP
> What do you think Errol?

> ERROL
> I think we should drip dry 'em guvner, while we got the chance.

The black guys start to struggle. Brick Top again frowns at Errol.

> BRICK TOP
> It was a rhetorical question Errol, what have I told you about thinking?

He turns back to the brothers.

> BRICK TOP (cont'd)
> You got forty-eight hours.

Pointing to Tyrone.

> BRICK TOP (cont'd)
> You can keep that silly fat wanker. The lads can't lift him. Forty-eight hours. After that it's your families, and the pigs finish what the dogs don't do.

INT. DOUG'S OFFICE – DAY

BULLET TOOTH TONY is sitting on a sofa flanked by Alex and Susi. In front of him are Doug, Avi and Rosebud.

                              AVI

So what should I call you? Should I call you Bullet?
Tooth?

                    BULLET TOOTH TONY (interrupting)
You can call me Susan if it makes you happy.

                              AVI

Tony. There is a man I'd like you to find.

                       BULLET TOOTH TONY
Well that depends on all the elements in the equation.
How many are there?

                              AVI

Forty thousand.

                       BULLET TOOTH TONY
Where was he last seen?

                              DOUG
At a bookie's.

                       BULLET TOOTH TONY
A bookie's? Pass us the blower, Susi.

Susi reaches for the phone.

EXT. HATTON GDN/DOUG'S SHOP – DAY

Bullet Tooth Tony, Avi and Rosebud leave Doug's shop and
walk to Bullet Tooth Tony's car.

BULLET TOOTH TONY

A bookie's got blagged last night.

AVI

Blagged? Speak English to me, Tony! I thought this
country spawned the fuckin' language and so far no
one seems to speak it.

BULLET TOOTH TONY

Blagged? Robbed. I gotta go and see a man who looks
like he might know something.

Rosebud interrupts.

ROSEBUD

I need a gun.

BULLET TOOTH TONY

No you don't, Rosebud me old son, you need me.

They all get into the car.

EXT. SEEDY STREET – DAY

Mullet is a seedy looking bloke, deep in conversation with
another horrible character as Bullet Tooth Tony's car pulls
up. He's extremely nervous about seeing Bullet Tooth Tony.

BULLET TOOTH TONY (interrupts)

All right Mullet?

MULLET

How ya doin' Tony? You all right mate?

BULLET TOOTH TONY
Nice tie.

It isn't.

MULLET
I heard you weren't about that much these days, Tone.

BULLET TOOTH TONY
Well. What do you know? Still warm the blood that courses through my veins. Unlike yours Mullet.

Pause.

BULLET TOOTH TONY (cont'd)
I want to know who blagged Brick Top's bookie's.

MULLET
Oh do me a favour, Tone.

BULLET TOOTH TONY
I will do you a favour, Mullet, I'll not bash the living fuck out of you in front of all your girlfriends here.

MULLET
Going to make it worth my while mate? Jesus, Tone, you know how it is, man.

Mullet nervously reaches forward. As quick as you like, Bullet Tooth Tony has Mullet by the collar and tie and pulls Mullet into the car. He then raises the electric window on Mullet's throat until it has fastened Mullet to the roof of the vehicle.

BULLET TOOTH TONY
Comfortable, Mullet? It seems sadly ironic it's that tie that's got you into this pickle.

Mullet has already gone pink.

BULLET TOOTH TONY (cont'd)
You take all the time you want mate.

Bullet Tooth Tony starts pulling away so Mullet has to keep walking along-side the car. Talking is not easy for Mullet in this situation and he sputters and chokes trying to get out his words.

MULLET
What the fuck you doin' Tone?

BULLET TOOTH TONY
I'm driving down the street with your head stuck in my window. What do you think I'm doing, you penis?

Bullet Tooth Tony does the window up a bit tighter. He pulls a face when he smells his breath.

BULLET TOOTH TONY
You been using dog shit for toothpaste Mullet?

Bullet Tooth Tony speeds up even more.

MULLET
Slow down, Tony. Slow down.

BULLET TOOTH TONY
Err, no I don't think I'll slow down. I think I'll speed up. I'll play you some music if you like.

Bullet Tooth Tony turns on the radio. A song comes on that he loves. (It's the same song from the flashback sequence in the topless bar.)

> BULLET TOOTH TONY (cont'd)
> Oh I love this track.

Pause.

> BULLET TOOTH TONY (cont'd)
> I want to know who blagged Brick Top's bookie's. Yes, Mullet?

> MULLET (strangled)
> I think it's two black guys who…work in a pawnshop in Smith Street.

> BULLET TOOTH TONY
> You better not be telling me porky pies –

> MULLET
> I'm fuckin' telling ya, it's two black guys who work out of a pawnshop on fucking Smith Street.

Bullet Tooth Tony loses interest but Mullet is still being dragged along.

> AVI
> It's very effective Tony. It's not too subtle, but effective. Are we taking him with us?

He points to Mullet. Bullet Tooth Tony pulls an, oh-yes-I-forgot-about-him face. He doesn't even look at Mullet. He lowers the window, and Mullet falls by the way, in God knows what condition.

INT. PAWNBROKER'S – DAY

The music from the previous scene ends abruptly as Sol speaks
– with some difficulty as his head is pinned to a table by Bullet
Tooth Tony with a gun. Avi is at Bullet Tooth Tony's side.

>   SOL
> It's the Russian.

>   AVI
> A Russian?

>   SOL
> Well to be technical he's an Uzbekistanian.

>   AVI
> Uzbekistanian? I've been dealing with those sneaky
> Russian dogs. (To Sol) Give me a name.

>   SOL
> Boris.

Bullet Tooth Tony looks familiar with the sound of this name.

>   BULLET TOOTH TONY
> Boris the Blade?

>   SOL
> Yeah.

>   BULLET TOOTH TONY
> As in Boris the Bullet Dodger?

AVI
Why do they call him the Bullet Dodger?

BULLET TOOTH TONY
Because he dodges bullets, Avi.

INT. BRICK TOP'S BOXING RING – DAY/
EXT. TURKISH'S BOXING RING – DAY

Brick Top is on the phone to Turkish, they are both in their own boxing rings. Turkish is nervous. We cut between the two scenes.

TURKISH
He won't fight unless we buy his mum a caravan. And you nicked all our savings.

BRICK TOP
In the quiet words of the Virgin Mary, 'come again'?

TURKISH
He's a stubborn bastard. He said he's got to look after his mum.

BRICK TOP
Are you taking the piss?

TURKISH
What can I do? I can't make him do it, can I?

BRICK TOP
You're not much good to me alive, are you Turkish?

Brick Top puts the phone down and inhales.

BRICK TOP (cont'd)
He's a useless shite that boy. Punish him for me, Errol. I
want that pikey to fight.

INT. AMUSEMENT ARCADE – NIGHT

There is music over this next section, and no live sound.

Turkish walks into the amusement arcade to find Brick Top's
men smashing everything up. The expression on Turkish's face
gets mean. He picks up a baseball bat and launches himself at
the men. He catches two off-guard but then is surrounded and
the bat taken out of his hands…As he's cornered, his voice-
over begins and continues over the next scene.

TURKISH (V/O)
Brick Top thought smashing up our arcade might help
me to persuade Mickey to fight. And if that wasn't
enough, he thought it would be a good idea to burn
Mickey's mum's caravan. While she was asleep in it.

EXT. CARAVAN CAMPSITE – NIGHT

Mickey, Darren, Patrick and various gypsies look at Mrs
O'Neil's caravan. It's engulfed in flames and all three are half
dressed and dirty from their efforts to save Mickey's mother.
Darren and Patrick restrain Mickey from hopeless attempts
to save her life as he tries to hurl himself into the flames.

No real sounds, only music.

INT. AMUSEMENT ARCADE – NIGHT

Music continues. Turkish is pinioned on the floor of the

amusement arcade. Errol raises a large blade to strike him. Just then Tommy, brandishing his gun, speaks and the music drops under the dialogue.

> TOMMY
> Turkish, get your arse up.

He directs his attention to the heavies.

> TOMMY (cont'd)
> You lot – you follow me, and I'll fuckin' shoot ya.

> ERROL
> Calm down son, behave yourself.

> TOMMY
> I've got the gun, son, I think it's you who should behave.

Errol steps forward, so does Tommy.

> TOMMY (cont'd)
> What? You want to see if I've got the minerals?

Tommy and Turkish moonwalk.

EXT. CARAVAN CAMPSITE – MORNING

Tommy and Turkish are looking at the burnt out caravan with Mickey. They are in shock.

> TURKISH
> Jesus, I'm sorry Mickey.

> MICKEY
> Did you do it?

Turkish and Tommy's eyes widen.

> MICKEY (cont'd)
> Then what are you sorry for?

Darren decides to interject. A woman shouts after him in the background.

> DARREN
> What the fuck are you two still doing here? You got some tars on ya?

Darren's eyes are full of poison. Tommy and Turkish suddenly feel very uncomfortable as Mickey tries to restrain Darren.

> MICKEY
> Fuck off, Darren. Fuck off.

Darren spins on his heel.

> TURKISH (V/O)
> How silly do I feel? His mum is still smoking next to us and I'm asking him to fight...

> MICKEY
> I'll do the fight before he causes any more carnage.

> TURKISH (V/O cont'd)
> ...and if he'd said no, it could have been a sight worse.

INT. DOUG'S OFFICE – DAY

Avi, Rosebud and Bullet Tooth Tony are back with Doug in his office.

AVI

Russians, hmmm, Russians, I should have known.
Anti-semite, slippery Cossack sluts. What do you
know about this gommum?

BULLET TOOTH TONY

Ex-KGB cancer. He was a highly trained undercover
agent. He'll be impossible to track down.

The phone rings. Doug picks it up. It's Susi who he can see
on the security monitor in the shop.

DOUG

Yeah

SUSI

Dad, there's a strange man down here who wants to
sell us an 84-carat stone.

DOUG

Where does he come from?

SUSI

I dunno. It's hard to tell. He's got a thick Russian
accent.

INT. PAWNBROKER'S – DAY

Brick Top and his men are long gone. Vin is scrubbing the
bloodstains off the floor, Tyrone is desperate to explain why
he gave them away.

TYRONE

Well, what was I supposed to do? He set the dogs on

me. Look.

He shows his wounds to Sol and Vin.

> VINNY
> That sneaky fuckin' Russian. No wonder he didn't want to do it.

> SOL
> First things first, one of us, Tyrone, you get round to the Russian's. The second you see him, you give us a call.

Pause. Tyrone does not move.

> SOL (cont'd)
> Now.

Tyrone gets up reluctantly.

INT. DOUG'S OFFICE – DAY

Avi, Rosebud, Doug and Bullet Tooth Tony are watching Boris on the security monitor. They're getting ready to move in.

> BULLET TOOTH TONY
> He's a right handful this fella, so watch out.

> ROSEBUD
> I hate Russians. I'll take care of him.

Avi and Bullet Tooth Tony look relieved for the offer.

BULLET TOOTH TONY
He's all yours Rosebud old son.

ROSEBUD
Not a problem.

Bullet Tooth Tony raises his eyebrows.

INT. BULLET TOOTH TONY'S CAR – DAY

The tone of the next few scenes is serious.

Bullet Tooth Tony is driving. Avi's in the front seat and
Rosebud is in the back. The latter's clutching his stomach
and his face is covered in blood, he is shouting and is
obviously in pain.

ROSEBUD
You're going to have to get me to a doctor. Shoot that
fuck! Then get me to a doctor.

AVI
Yeah, yeah but first we get the stone, Rosey, first the
stone, and then I'll get you to a doctor, and not just any
doctor, boychick, I'm going to get you to a nice Jewish
doctor. (To Bullet Tooth Tony) Find my friend a nice
Jewish doctor!

CUT TO:

EXT. BORIS'S HOUSE – DAY

Bullet Tooth Tony and Rosebud pull Boris up out of the car
boot. He has a bag over his head. Rosebud puts a blade to

the Russian's neck. Tyrone who is hanging around looking out for Boris, witnesses this.

> BULLET TOOTH TONY
> Get his keys and find out exactly where the stone is.

> ROSEBUD
> I think that you've got something to tell us.

> AVI
> Easy. Take it easy Rosebud.

Bullet Tooth Tony looks at the blood that is already starting to pierce the skin from where the blade is pressed against the Russian's neck. Bullet Tooth Tony then looks at Avi with concern.

> BULLET TOOTH TONY
> Oi, do you want him to be able to talk or not?

INT. PAWNBROKER'S – DAY

Sol is waving two pistols in front of Vinny.

> VINNY
> What the fuck do you mean, replicas?

> SOL
> They look the shit don't they? Nobody is gonna argue.
> And I've got some extra loud blanks just in case.

> VINNY
> Oh, in case we have to deafen them to death?

Sol's phone rings. Sol gives the guns to Vinny who looks at them in disbelief, and answers the phone.

                    SOL (cont'd)
          Yeah?

EXT. BORIS'S HOUSE – DAY

Tyrone is in a phone box outside Boris's house.

                    TYRONE
          Boris is here.

INT. PAWNBROKER'S – DAY

Sol is on the phone to Tyrone.

                    SOL
          We're coming over. You hold him there.

Sol puts the phone down before he has to hear what Tyrone has to say.

EXT. BORIS'S HOUSE – DAY

Tyrone is still on the phone although Sol has hung up.

                    TYRONE
          (continuing after Sol's put the phone down)
          Hold on!....He's not on his own!

Tyrone's looking at Bullet Tooth Tony, Avi and Rosebud bundle Boris back into the boot of the car and head into the house.

INT. PAWNBROKER'S – DAY – CONTINUOUS

Sol whips a gun from Vinny's hand.

> SOL
>
> We're off!

INT. BORIS'S HOUSE – DAY

Bullet Tooth Tony, Avi and Rosebud are crouched over a
sunken safe. There are lots of valuables including the case.

> AVI
>
> Very industrious for a Cossack.

Avi rifles through the case and finds the diamond.

> AVI (cont'd)
>
> Sneaky fuckin' Russian.

EXT. BORIS'S HOUSE – DAY

We cut to Vinny and Sol tearing round to Boris's. They're
driving Tyrone's car, and the dog is with them. The car
screeches to a halt and Tyrone approaches.

> SOL
>
> So where is he, Tyrone?

> TYRONE
>
> It's not just a he, three fellas went in the house and they
> locked Boris in the back of the car.

                    SOL
Why didn't you tell us that?

Tyrone pulls a 'I tried' face.

                    VINNY
Oi, did they look hard?

                    TYRONE
They look messy.

INT. BORIS'S HOUSE – DAY – CONTINUOUS

                    AVI
OK, come on, let's get out of here.

                BULLET TOOTH TONY
What do you want to do about the Russian?

                    AVI
I want you to bury him.

                BULLET TOOTH TONY
All right.

INT. TURKISH'S CAR – CONTINUOUS

Turkish and Tommy are in the car – Tommy is driving.
Turkish is drinking a pint of milk (as usual). There is silence
for a while.

                    TURKISH
I think we should get you a new gun, Tommy, but this
time, try it.

TOMMY
How far to the Russian's?

TURKISH
We'll be there in a minute.

He takes a sip of his milk and accidentally spills a little.

EXT. BORIS'S HOUSE – DAY

Avi, Tony and Rosebud walk out.

EXT. TYRONE'S CAR/EXT. BORIS'S HOUSE – DAY

The three black guys witness this. Tyrone is now in the front seat driving.

VINNY (cont'd)
Well come on then.

SOL
Nah, not so fast Vinny, we can't take 'em now, we're gonna have to follow 'em.

INT. TURKISH'S CAR – CONTINUOUS

Conversation continues.

TOMMY
(gesturing to milk)
Shouldn't drink that stuff anyway.

TURKISH
Why, what's wrong with it?

TOMMY
It's not in sync with evolution...

TURKISH
Shut up!

INT. BULLET TOOTH TONY'S CAR – DAY

The car moves off.

AVI
How do you wanna get rid of him?

BULLET TOOTH TONY
Well, do you wanna shoot him?

AVI
It's a little noisy isn't it?

BULLET TOOTH TONY
Do you wanna stab him?

AVI
It's a little coldblooded, isn't it?

BULLET TOOTH TONY
D'you wanna kill him or not?

ROSEBUD
I'll cut him. I gotta blade.

BULLET TOOTH TONY
Yeah, that's the spirit.

Rosebud pulls out a knife.

INT. TYRONE'S CAR – DAY

Tyrone, Sol and Vinny follow Bullet Tooth Tony's car in theirs.

> VINNY
>
> Do they fire?

Pointing to the guns.

> SOL
>
> Of course they fire.

> VINNY
>
> Yeah but how do you know? They're replicas, what do
> you know about replicas?

Sol looks at the gun and frowns, 'what does he know about
replicas'? He pulls the trigger.

EXT. TYRONE'S CAR – LONDON STREET –
CONTINUOUS

There is a flash, and a very loud bang, all the windows
shatter. The car does a massive swerve and everything nearly
ends in disaster, Tyrone regains control of the car.

INT. TYRONE'S CAR – CONTINUOUS

Everyone is shouting.

> VINNY
>
> What the fuck are you doing Solomon?!!

SOL
Well you wanted to know whether or not they worked!

VINNY
I didn't mean try it in the car, Sol, you arsehole!

Suddenly, there is a loud smash and a body crashes into the windshield.

INT. BULLET TOOTH TONY'S CAR – DAY

Bullet Tooth Tony isn't impressed with Rosebud's knife.

BULLET TOOTH TONY (cont'd)
What are you going to do with that? Pick his teeth?
Wipe the butter off it and put it away.

Bullet Tooth Tony points behind the passenger seat.

BULLET TOOTH TONY
Look, there's a proper blade back there.

INT. TURKISH'S CAR – CONTINUOUS

Conversation continues.

TOMMY
Cows have only been domesticated in the last eight thousand years. Before that they were running around mad as lorries. The human digestive system hasn't got used to any dairy products yet.

TURKISH
Well fuck me Tommy, what have you been reading?

Tommy looks back at him.

TOMMY
Let me do you a favour.

He reaches over and grabs the carton from Turkish, and throws it out the window. There is a terrible crashing noise. The milk has obviously hit an on-coming car in the other direction. They look back to see what's happened.

TOMMY AND TURKISH
Whoops.

INT. BULLET TOOTH TONY's CAR – DAY

Conversation continues.

BULLET TOOTH TONY (to Avi)
You, you want a knife?

AVI
Me? No, I wouldn't know what to do with it.

BULLET TOOTH TONY
It's a knife for God's sake. What have you used to keep your fork company all these years?

Avi slowly turns to look behind and sees Rosebud attempting to pull a bloody great sword out of its scabbard.

BULLET TOOTH TONY (cont'd)
A sharp side, a blunt side. What do you want, a lesson?

There is a sudden bang on the windshield and Bullet Tooth

Tony turns back to the front only to see the windshield covered in milk. The car swerves to the side of the road and hits a post. They crash. Fade out.

EXT. BULLET TOOTH TONY'S CAR – CONTINUOUS

We start on black. Muffled and kicking sounds are heard and swearing in Russian, then light appears. We are clearly with Boris in the boot.

INT. BULLET TOOTH TONY'S CAR– CONTINUOUS

Bullet Tooth Tony and Avi are covered in blood. Bullet Tooth Tony lifts his head up from the steering wheel. Avi slowly opens his eyes and turns in Bullet Tooth Tony's direction. He turns to see a man with a bag over his head with his hands tied up wandering around somewhat unconfidently in the middle of the road.

                              AVI
        Is that Boris?

All of a sudden a car (Tyrone's) hits Boris and he is bounced off the windshield and onto the road. The car screeches to a halt.

INT. TYRONE'S CAR – CONTINUOUS

The black guys are in shock.

                              SOL
        Oh Tyrone, what have you done?!

INT BULLET TOOTH TONY'S CAR – CONTINUOUS

                    AVI
What about Rosebud?

              BULLET TOOTH TONY
Well, you can bring him with you if you like, but which
bit would you like to bring?

The sword has sliced right through Rosebud in the back
seat. As Bullet Tooth Tony and Avi emerge from the car, a
crowd of Asian women start to gather.

INT. TYRONE'S CAR – CONTINUOUS

The black guys are hiding in their car, holding replicas.

                   VINNY
They're getting out.

                    SOL
Get down and follow them.

EXT. LONDON STREET – DAY

Bullet Tooth Tony and Avi, sprinkled in blood, get out of the
car and start walking. They push their way through the
gathering crowd.

              BULLET TOOTH TONY
Cover yourself up Avi. You're making a scene.

                    AVI
I'm sorry for causing a scene, Tony.

EXT. PUB – DAY

The three black guys are still in the car, waiting to follow Bullet Tooth Tony and Avi and are readying themselves for action.

> SOL
> Whoa! You are not taking that dog with you Vince!

> VINNY
> Well, I can't leave him in here, can I?

Sol rolls his eyes.

EXT. PUB – CONTINUOUS

Bullet Tooth Tony and Avi, briefcase in hand, stop and enter a pub.

INT. PUB – CONTINUOUS

Bullet Tooth Tony goes to the payphone to call Doug, and Avi follows.

> BULLET TOOTH TONY
> Pint of the black stuff, landlord. (To Avi) I thought you wanted to get cleaned up. Bathroom's back there.

Avi leaves for the bathroom as Bullet Tooth Tony makes his call.

EXT. BORIS'S HOUSE – DAY

Tommy and Turkish are standing outside Boris's house.

TURKISH

He's left the door open.

TOMMY

Shouldn't think that's a good idea. Shall we go in?

TURKISH

I don't want to go in there. He's a dangerous bastard, taken too many disco biscuits in the heat of Russian disputations. He's got as many of these nuts as he has those nuts.

He grabs his groin and points to his temple.

TOMMY

I don't care if he's got fuckin' hazelnuts, I want a gun that works, and I'm gonna tell him.

TURKISH

My God, Tommy, you certainly got those minerals. Come on then, before 'ze Germans' get here. You just tell him who's in charge.

Boris comes round the corner covered in blood and swearing in Russian. Tommy protests to the blood-stained Russian.

TOMMY

Er, Boris…

The Cossack picks Tommy up by the bollocks, and walks him to the wall. Boris marches into the house and slams the door shut behind him.

TURKISH
You certainly told him Tommy.

Boris re-emerges, still muttering, and carrying a grenade launcher as Turkish and Tommy (still crumpled on the floor) look on.

INT. PUB (cont'd)

BULLET TOOTH TONY
…the Drowning Trout. Come and pick us up. And Doug, sharpish.

As he speaks Sol, Vinny and Tyrone enter the pub wearing balaclavas. They go straight over to Bullet Tooth Tony and point a gun to the back of his head. Despite seeing the barman's disappeared, Bullet Tooth Tony seems unaware that they are there until he sits down with his pint.

SOL
I don't want a fuss and I don't want to put a bullet in your face, but unless you give me exactly what I want, there will be fuckin' murders.

Sol cocks the gun and Bullet Tooth Tony pulls a sarcastic 'I am shocked' face.

BULLET TOOTH TONY
What's your name?

VINNY
Shoot him!

Sol goes to hit him with the gun, but it's caught by Bullet Tooth

Tony. Sol tries to pull the nose of the gun out of Bullet Tooth
Tony's hand, but he can't move it. Vinny steps forward and
raises his gun.

<blockquote>
VINNY
LET. GO. OF. THE. GUN.
</blockquote>

Bullet Tooth Tony lets go, Sol gathers himself and Vinny and
Sol both point their guns at Bullet Tooth Tony.

<blockquote>
BULLET TOOTH TONY
...So, you're obviously the big dick, and that, on either
side of you, are your balls. There are two types of balls,
there are big brave balls and there are little mincey
faggot balls...
</blockquote>

<blockquote>
VINNY
These are your last words so make them a prayer.
</blockquote>

<blockquote>
BULLET TOOTH TONY
Now dicks have drive, and clarity of vision...but
they're not clever, they smell pussy, and they want a piece
of the action. And you thought you smelt gooood ol
pussy, and have brought your two little mincey faggot
balls along for a gooood ol' time, but you have got your
parties muddled up, there's no pussy here, just a dose
that'll make you wish you were born a woman.
</blockquote>

We cut to the brothers. They are looking confused and uneasy.

<blockquote>
BULLET TOOTH TONY (cont'd)
Like a prick, you're having second thoughts: you're
shrinking, and your two little balls are shrinking with
you. And the fact that you've got 'REPLICA' written
</blockquote>

down the side of your gun...

The camera smashes into a close-up of the gun that Sol is holding. We clearly see a bold 'REPLICA' written down the side.

> BULLET TOOTH TONY (cont'd)
> ...And the fact that I've got 'Desert Eagle .50'...written on the side of mine...

He calmly places the GUN on the table in front of him. Camera smashes into 'DESERT EAGLE .50' written down the side.

> BULLET TOOTH TONY (cont'd)
> ...should precipitate your balls in shrinking along with your presence.

The brothers have lost this one and they know it.

> BULLET TOOTH TONY
> Now. Fuck off.

Bullet Tooth Tony takes a sip of the black stuff as the trio back away into the corridor down to the back door of the pub.

INT. CORRIDOR – CONTINUOUS

> VINNY (to Tyrone)
> Lock the door! Lock it!

As they lock the door of the corridor Avi appears from the bathroom, drying his hands. He's got the case in his arms. The brothers adapt to their new scenario:
Sol and Vinny arm their guns and threaten Avi.

                          VINNY
      Give me the case!

Avi clutches his briefcase and is defiant.

                           AVI
      Fuck you! Shoot me.

                          VINNY
      I will. I'll shoot ya.

Vinny readies the gun .

INT. PUB – CONTINUOUS

Bullet Tooth Tony's on the other side of the wall. He can
hear that the black guys and Avi have run into each other.

INT. CORRIDOR – CONTINUOUS

At this moment of the stand-off, the door at the other end of
the corridor opens – and Boris comes in waving his grenade
launcher at Avi and the black guys.

                          BORIS
      Pass my case. Or I shoot you.

Avi is still clutching the case.

                           AVI
      You know what? Fuck you too.

INT. PUB – CONTINUOUS

Bullet Tooth Tony makes his way towards the corridor.

INT. CORRIDOR – CONTINUOUS

> AVI
> Go ahead and do me…you'd be doing me a favour you
> Russian fuck. Go ahead!

Boris turns to Sol and Vinny.

> BORIS
> You! Drop guns!

Vinny, in turn, keeps his gun firmly pointed at Boris.

> VINNY
> Fuck you!

INT. PUB – CONTINUOUS

Bullet Tooth Tony tries the handle of the corridor. It's locked.

INT. CORRIDOR – CONTINUOUS

Boris prepares himself to shoot the black guys.

> BORIS
> OK!

Bullet Tooth Tony's voice is heard.

BULLET TOOTH TONY
                    Avi?

INT. PUB – CONTINUOUS

Bullet Tooth Tony aims his gun at the wall and shouts.

                    BULLET TOOTH TONY
                    Pull your socks up!

INT. CORRIDOR – CONTINUOUS

There's a pause as Avi realises what's going on, then he dives
to the floor. The black guys, intent on the case, dive after
him, leaving Tyrone and Boris standing. Bullets start to thud
through the plaster – hitting Boris first of all.

INT. PUB – CONTINUOUS

Bullet Tooth Tony shoots methodically through the wall.

INT. CORRIDOR – CONTINUOUS

Bullets fly through the wall. Tyrone falls to the floor as
bullets go past him.

INT. PUB – CONTINUOUS

Bullet Tooth Tony stops firing.

INT. CORRIDOR – CONTINUOUS

Boris is slumped against the wall groaning. Sol turns round
to check on Tyrone.

SOL

Tyrone?

VINNY

Fuck it! We're out of here!

Sol and Vinny scramble up with the case and make a break for it through the door at the end of the corridor. Boris weakly tries to stop them.

BORIS

Give me the case!

The door from the pub into the corridor crashes open and Bullet Tooth Tony appears, surveying the carnage. He loads a new round into his gun and walks down to Avi.

BULLET TOOTH TONY

Avi? Where's the case?

AVI

Put the gun away!

Bullet Tooth Tony notices Boris struggling in the corner.

BULLET TOOTH TONY

What's Boris doing here? Boris, what are you doing here?

BORIS (muffled)

Fuck you!

Bullet Tooth Tony fires two shots at Boris. He walks up towards Tyrone who is cowering.

           BULLET TOOTH TONY (to TYRONE)
Where's the case?

                    BORIS
Ha! You missed!

              BULLET TOOTH TONY
Don't take the piss, Boris.

                    BORIS
I'll show…you…

Bullet Tooth Tony cocks his gun and fires four shots.

                    BORIS
Fuck you!

Bullet Tooth Tony fires another shot.

                    BORIS
…Almost!…

              BULLET TOOTH TONY
Fuck's sake!

Bullet Tooth Tony fires another shot. There's a whimper and
no more noise out of Boris.

INT. PUB – CONTINUOUS

           BULLET TOOTH TONY (To TYRONE)
Fuck you, an' all.

Bullet Tooth Tony aims the gun at Tyrone, and turns away

to avoid the blast. But it just clicks. It's out of bullets.

                    BULLET TOOTH TONY
          You lucky bastard!

INT. PAWNBROKER'S – DAY

Vinny is holding the diamond. They are back in the office
and the dog's barking and squeaking again.

                    VINNY
          Jesus, it's flawless.

                    SOL
          Don't get attached to it, it's going to Brick Top. Leave
          the dog here.

                    VINNY
          So, why don't we just…leave?

                    SOL
          Because life's too short Vincent, and it'll get a lot
          fuckin' shorter if Brick Top wishes it to be. Now leave
          that dog here.

                    VINNY
          I'm gonna leave the dog here, don't worry about it.

                    SOL
          If that pikey mutt does any damage, you're gonna pay.

                    VINNY (to the dog)
          Sit down!

They leave the dog in the back room.

EXT. BRICK TOP'S PUB – DAY

Vinny and Sol are sitting in the car outside Brick Top's, psyching themselves up for the encounter ahead of them.

> VINNY
> I don't wanna go in there. You'll never see me again.

> SOL
> Well, we won't, if you don't. All right, you give me the stone and I will give it to Brick Top. Yeah?

> VINNY
> All right. Give me a minute. It's a bit fiddly.

Vinny undoes his jacket and starts to feel in his trousers. Sol looks concerned.

> SOL
> What is it doing down there?

> VINNY
> Well, I put it down there in case we got mugged.

> SOL
> You ain't from this planet, are you Vincent? Who is gonna mug two black fellas, holding pistols, sat in a car that's worth less than your shirt?

> VINNY
> (looking through the window)
> Bullet Tooth Tony and his friend Desert Eagle .50.

                    SOL
        What have they gotta do with anything?

Bullet Tooth Tony's reflection approaches on Sol's window.

                    VINNY
        They're both staring straight at me.

They turn to look out of Sol's window. Bullet Tooth Tony
taps on the window with his gun.

                BULLET TOOTH TONY
        You should never underestimate the predictability of
        stupidity. Now outta the car. And leave your water
        pistols behind.

Sol puts his hands up.

                    VINNY
        Look, just tell him the stone's back at the office. I'll
        think of something.

INT. TURKISH'S CARAVAN

Turkish, Tommy and Gorgeous George are playing cards in
their caravan. Gorgeous is bandaged and wearing a head
brace. Tommy loses another hand.

                    TURKISH
        Why's he sweating, Gorgeous?

Gorgeous George mumbles incoherently through his brace.

TURKISH

Tommy, why's your skin leaking?

TOMMY

I'm a little worried actually, Turkish.

TURKISH

Worried about what?

TOMMY

What happens if the gypsy knocks the other man out? I
mean, he's done it before inn'he?

TURKISH

We get murdered before we leave the building. And I
imagine we get fed to the pigs.

Turkish puts down another card calmly.

TOMMY

Well, I'm glad you're climbing the walls in fuckin'
anxiety. Pardon my cynicism, but I don't exactly trust
the pikey.

TURKISH

Don't think I haven't thunk about that one, Tommy.

As Turkish speaks, we cut to see scenes of Mum O'Neil's
funeral and wake. Mickey is clearly in mourning.

TURKISH (cont'd)

It's his mum's funeral tonight, God bless her. Y'know
how those gypsies like a drink at a wake. Not worried
about whether Mickey knocks the other man out.

Worried about whether Mickey makes it to the fourth fuckin' round.

Intercut with scenes of the wake. Mickey's clearly been drinking.

> TOMMY
> Well, what if he doesn't make it to the fourth round?

> TURKISH
> We get murdered before we leave the building. And I imagine we get fed to the pigs.

Tommy throws down his cards.

> TOMMY
> So why are you so calm?

Pause.

> TOMMY (cont'd)
> I said...

Turkish loses his temper.

> TURKISH
> I heard what you said Tommy! It's not as though we've got a choice now, is it? You show me how to control a wild fuckin' gypsy and I'll show you how to control an unhinged, pig-feeding gangster.

Turkish throws down his cards.

                    TURKISH
          Bollocks! I'm going for a walk!

Turkish storms out.

EXT. CARAVAN CAMPSITE/INT. BARN – DAY

We return to the wake. There is music over the entire scene.
It is obvious that a lot of hardcore drinking has been going
on. Drunk and dishevelled, Mickey is at the centre of the
funeral revelry. It's a strangely sad scene because there
appears to be laughter involved with the mourning.

INT. PAWNBROKER'S – NIGHT

Avi and Bullet Tooth Tony have Vinny and Sol in tow. They
enter the back room. It's a complete mess. They all grimace
at the smell. The dog comes running up, looking extremely
relieved to see someone.

                        SOL
          Fuckin' dog. Go on get the dog.

                  BULLET TOOTH TONY
          Bit funky in here, innit?

Bullet Tooth Tony and Avi hold their noses.

                  AVI (to BULLET TOOTH TONY)
          Open the window.

Bullet Tooth Tony opens a window.

                    AVI
You people live like animals. Now where's the stone?
Come on, where it is?

                    VINNY
It's over here.

Vinny points to a mess in the corner. There are papers and
jewellery boxes littered everywhere.

                    AVI
Where? Where?

Vinny starts to look for the box.

                    VINNY
I left it in a box...

Vinny and Sol rifle through some things and Vinny retrieves
an empty box.

                    VINNY (cont'd)
It's empty.

Avi is clearly distressed by the news.

                    AVI
I'm getting heartburn. Tony, do something terrible.

                    VINNY
No! I'm being serious...the dog. The dog must have
had it.

All eyes focus on the dog.

                              AVI
          Well then, let's have a look shall we? Tony?

All eyes focus on Bullet Tooth Tony.

                    BULLET TOOTH TONY
        What?

                              AVI
        Look in the dog.

                    BULLET TOOTH TONY
        What do you mean, 'look in the dog'?

                              AVI
        I mean: open him up.

Bullet Tooth Tony is not sure about this.

                    BULLET TOOTH TONY
        It's not a fuckin' tin of baked beans. What d'you mean:
        'open him up'?

                              AVI
        You know what I mean.

                    BULLET TOOTH TONY
        That's a bit strong innit?

Bullet Tooth Tony looks completely unsure about this and
rocks his head from side to side but resigns himself to his
duty and takes his coat off.

VINNY

No, you can't do this.

Bullet Tooth Tony has a knife in his mouth and holds down
the dog. The dog starts to squeak.

BULLET TOOTH TONY

It's fuckin' squeaking.

AVI

You never heard a dog squeak before?...Give me the
goddam dog!

Avi points the gun at the dog. Vinny and Sol try to intervene.
The dog is barking and running around, general mayhem
ensues. The dog goes for Vinny and Sol and eventually
Vinny pulls the diamond from out of his trousers.

AVI

You sneaky fuckin' bastard.

Avi sits down to examine the stone. He looks at Bullet Tooth
Tony with relief and joy.

BULLET TOOTH TONY

Thank God for that.

At this point the dog leaps up, grabs the stone in its mouth
from Avi's hand and swallows it whole. Avi pulls his gun
and begins shooting wildly round the room at the dog as the
dog leaps through the open window. Avi legs it to the
window and shoots at the disappearing dog.

                              AVI
          I hate fuckin' dogs! Come on Tony!

Avi runs out of the office. Bullet Tooth Tony does not follow.
Avi turns back.

                              AVI
              Tony, come on!

Avi stops, realising that he's shot Bullet Tooth Tony by
accident.

Travel montage in reverse.
CUT TO: British black cab door slamming
CUT TO: Avi taking pills on plane
CUT TO: Concorde takes off
CUT TO: Passport being stamped
CUT TO: Avi in New York customs.

            CUSTOMS OFFICER (off camera)
          Anything to declare?

                              AVI
          Yeah. Don't go to England.

CUT TO: New York cab light going off.

INT. PAWNBROKER'S – NIGHT

Sol and Vinny are carrying Bullet Tooth Tony's body out of
the back office.

                              VIN
          That dog is gonna go back to the campsite Sol, I'm
          telling you it always does.

SOL

How's the dog gonna find the campsite then?

VIN

Have you smelt the campsite, Sol?

SOL

All right. But we're gonna have to wait until it gets light.
And we have got to get rid of these bodies. That one over
there with a tea cosy over his head is starting to stink.

VIN

Right, let's stick them in the car and then go and look
for a pig farm.

Vin and Sol go to dispose of the bodies.

INT. WAREHOUSE BACK ROOM – DRESSING ROOM

Tommy and Turkish are standing over someone.

TURKISH

Oi, Mickey.

Turkish wakes Mickey up. He was having a kip on the sofa.

TURKISH (cont'd)

You feeling all right Mickey?

MICKEY (slurring)

Need a drink!

Turkish grabs the whisky flask out of Tommy's jacket.

TOMMY

You can't give him a drink.

TURKISH

It's not for him, it's for me.

Turkish takes a swig and hands it to a grateful Mickey who takes a swig. Mickey mumbles. Tommy takes a swig.

TURKISH

He's a hard bastard this 'Good Night' Anderson, so pay attention to what you're doing.

Pause. Mickey's asleep again.

TURKISH (cont'd)

All right Mickey?

Turkish slaps Mickey to wake him up.

TURKISH (cont'd)

Mickey?

Mickey sits up and mumbles drunkenly.

MICKEY

Need to have a shite!

EXT. WAREHOUSE – NIGHT

Brick Top is sitting in the back of a car with three of his heavies including Errol.

> BRICK TOP
> If you see the pikey, Turkish or his girlfriend come out
> before me, shoot the bastards!

Errol nods.

> BRICK TOP (cont'd)
> Well, come on, we've got a fight to go to.

INT. WAREHOUSE – NIGHT

A temporary RING has been erected, four scaffolding posts
with welded-on hoops make the arena, the ropes that are
threaded through the hoops are industrial nylon and free of
padding. Around the ropes it's starting to fill. Brick Top
approaches Salt Peter and Jack the All Seeing Eye.

> SALT PETER
> I hope we're gonna get a fuckin' better show this time.

> BRICK TOP
> This will make up for it. Mickey's going down in the
> fourth. Now Terry over there is in charge of the bets.
> Now (moving on), you'll have to forgive me.

> JACK THE ALL SEEING EYE (interrupts)
> I'll forgive you if he goes down this time.

Brick Top moves on with Errol.

> BRICK TOP (cont'd)
> Are our lads down at the campsite?

ERROL

They're over there now, guv'nor.

EXT. CARAVAN CAMPSITE – NIGHT

CUT TO: a shot of some of Brick Top's heavies waiting in
two vans outside the gypsy campsite.

HEAVY 1

I fuckin' hate pikeys.

HEAVY 2

How long have we gotta stay here?

HEAVY 3

As long as it takes, now shut up.

HEAVY 1

I fuckin' hate pikeys.

INT. BACK OF WAREHOUSE – NIGHT

Brick Top is standing in front of Mickey whose eyes are still
semi-open. Errol, Turkish and Tommy are also there.
Tommy is tying boxing bandages around Mickey's hands.

BRICK TOP

Is he fuckin' stoned?

TURKISH

He's like that before a fight.

He turns his attention to Mickey.

                    BRICK TOP
Do you know when you're going down?

                    TURKISH
Of course he knows when he's going down...

                    ERROL
Oi, fuck face, who's speaking to you? He asked him,
didn't he?

                    TURKISH
Fuck face? I like that one Errol, I'll have to remember
that one next time I'm climbing off your mum.

                BRICK TOP (intervenes)
Not now.

Mickey's response is incoherent but he's laughing to himself.
It's certainly not the response Brick Top is looking for.

                    BRICK TOP
There's a campsite full of pikeys that might not think
you're so fuckin' funny. Not when they are putting out
the flames on their children's backs.

Pause. The atmosphere changes.

                BRICK TOP (cont'd)
Now get out there and have a fucking fight.

INT. WAREHOUSE

Mickey appears from a small door at the back of the
warehouse. He's wearing a pair of trousers, white T-shirt, a

shirt and his trademark hat. Turkish walks in front of him, Tommy behind. Mickey approaches the ring accompanied by shouts of encouragement and counter shouts. He responds to the counter shouts and gets involved in a skirmish. Turkish and Tommy pull him away only for him to dive in again. Finally, Mickey enters the ring. Horace 'Good Night' Anderson, is already there. He is a big guy with a nose that appears to have seen countless rounds with a frying pan. Mickey passes his shirt, T-shirt and hat to Tommy. Both fighters limber up, throw a few shadow punches. They meet in the middle with the ref.

REFEREE
I'm in charge here. I want no fuckin' about. No eye gouging. Do your worst. Let's get it on.

The two fighters pace one another for a second or two then 'Good Night' advances on Mickey who lets one of his missiles go. Bang – it shakes Good Night to his core and over he goes. Tommy and Turkish wince and Brick Top and Errol look serious. Mickey backs away and feints around the ring while Good Night gets up.

REFEREE (to Mickey)
What the fuck's going on…You going to finish him or what?

Good Night advances on Mickey again. They exchange a few punches then it gets serious and they go at it, hammer and tongs. The camera speeds up and an onslaught of punches is exchanged until Good Night gets knocked down again. As he gets up, the bell goes. They go back to their separate corners.

TURKISH
Talk about saved by the bell. Do you understand the

consequences of what would happen if you knocked that man out? Do not knock him out, Mickey.

The bell goes again and Mickey prepares himself for the second round. This time he backs away from the bloodied Good Night who chases him round the ring. The bell goes again as Mickey's knocked to his knees and blood spurts from his face – and we go into super slow motion as the two fighters start to seriously damage each other…punches are slowed down, blood flies and as the bell goes again, Good Night has backed Mickey into the ropes where he is methodically hitting him and does not immediately stop.

TURKISH

What, is he fucking deaf?

Turkish and Tommy, along with Good Night's trainers jump into the ring and start having a go at each other. Mickey slides down the ropes, seemingly exhausted, then slowly gets up. Turkish takes him back to his corner.

TURKISH

What the fuck are you doing Mickey? You're dancing like a fairy! They'll hang us with the ring ropes if they think it's rigged. Get out there and hurt him. For fuck's sake, do not knock him out.

Mickey rises, bloodied. Good Night paces on the other side. They approach each other. Mickey's hands are low, BANG, there's a flash of white as Good Night gets in a good right hook. Mickey squares up, Good Night ducks and gets in a good left hook – BANG, another white flash. Mickey hits the floor. Brick Top and Errol shift uneasily, Turkish and Tommy exchange looks – but then Mickey rises, slowly,

211

painfully. He's stumbling, looking lost. Good Night gets in a flurry of big punches and finally catches Mickey under the chin and he flies up and backwards down onto the canvas… WE GO INTO A BLACK AND WHITE FANTASY SEQUENCE.

When Mickey hits the deck he goes through the dust-covered floor like it's made of water. He falls through the dark water, sinks; his eyes are open and he can't breath but he's unpanicked, looking around. Looking up, he can see through the floor of the ring – Good Night kicking his body around but he's unbothered, seemingly waiting…
Back in the ring, Good Night is standing over Mickey's body. Is it over? The latter's eyes open slowly…

TURKISH (V/O)
All he's got to do is stay down…

Mickey's eyes continue to open. There's a flash of him underwater gathering himself for a punch and then…he leaps to his feet in the ring and lands a definitive punch to Good Night's jaw. The scene freezes.

TURKISH (V/O)
Now, we are fucked.

The scene unfreezes and a surprised Good Night topples to the canvas. He's out cold. The ref tries to revive him but it's clearly all over. The crowd goes mad. Brick Top turns to Errol.

BRICK TOP
We're out of here.

Turkish and Tommy jump into the ring and pull Mickey out.

TURKISH

Stupid fuckin' pikey knows Brick Top's got a dozen
keen-to-kill monkeys with shotguns sitting outside his
campsite.

EXT. WAREHOUSE – NIGHT

Brick Top is outside the warehouse on his mobile phone. A shot
is heard. Brick Top slams his mobile shut and turns to Errol.

TURKISH (V/O)

Once the campsite is wiped out, I know it's going to be
the same for us.

Brick Top turns to see Turkish, Tommy and Mickey stumbling
down the steps to the car from the warehouse. They haven't
seen Brick Top – Brick Top taps the window of his waiting car.

TURKISH (V/O)

Have you ever crossed the road and looked the wrong
way…

INT. BRICK TOP'S CAR OUTSIDE WAREHOUSE –
NIGHT

BRICK TOP
(to the men in his car)
Give me that fuckin' shooter!

EXT. WAREHOUSE

Turkish, Tommy and Mickey have now realised Brick Top is
there.

> TURKISH (V/O cont'd)
> …and hey presto, there's nearly a car on ya?…

INT. BRICK TOP'S CAR OUTSIDE WAREHOUSE –
NIGHT

Car window begins to slide down.

> TURKISH (V/O cont'd)
> …So what do you do?…

The screen goes black.

> TURKISH (V/O cont'd)
> …Something very silly…

There is the sound of a gunshot over the black.

EXT. WAREHOUSE – NIGHT

Freeze frame of Turkish, Mickey and Tommy. Turkish and
Tommy, reacting to something, look petrified. Mickey is
standing unmoved.

> TURKISH (V/O cont'd)
> …You freeze. Your life doesn't flash before you
> because you're too fuckin' scared to think. You just
> freeze and pull a stupid face. The pikey didn't. Why?
> Because he had plans on running the car over…

EXT. CARAVAN CAMPSITE – NIGHT – FLASHBACK

There's a close-up of Mickey's face watching his mother's
caravan burning.

> TURKISH (V/O cont'd)
> …It had previously occurred to me that the gypsy had taken the demise of his mother rather lightly…

EXT. CAMPSITE – NIGHT

Guns are being loaded. We see Darren and a line of gypsies with their guns poised.

> TURKISH (V/O cont'd)
> …For every action, there is a reaction. And a pikey reaction…

INT. BRICK TOP'S HENCHMAN'S VAN AT CAMPSITE – NIGHT

The camera crashes into a close-up of one of Brick Top's drivers at the wheel. He looks out of the van and sees the pikeys approach.

> TURKISH (V/O cont'd)
> …is quite a fuckin' thing.

EXT. CAMPSITE – CONTINUOUS

The music comes back on. The gypsies let rip. A hail of bullets hit the two Brick Top vans.

INT. WAREHOUSE

Good Night goes down again. Intercut with the massacre of Brick Top's men by the gypsies.

EXT. WAREHOUSE – NIGHT

One of Mickey's men taps on the window of Brick Top's car and then shoots through it. On the other side of the car, Brick Top's other man is being strangled by another gypsy.

INT. WAREHOUSE – NIGHT – FLASHBACK

Turkish is pulling Mickey out of the ring. The flashback continues. The crowd discovers its own disputes. Chairs start to fly. Brick Top's men are prevented from reaching Turkish, Tommy and Mickey by the mayhem.

EXT. CAMPSITE – NIGHT

Pete, one of Brick Top's henchmen, is crawling on his stomach through the darkness. He is wounded.

EXT. WAREHOUSE – NIGHT – FLASHBACK

As previously, Brick Top is on his mobile phone outside the warehouse after the fight.

EXT. CAMPSITE – NIGHT

Pete turns onto his back. His mobile phone rings. A shotgun is put to Pete's neck and a hand removes the phone.

EXT. WAREHOUSE – NIGHT – FLASHBACK

This time we hear Brick Top's conversation.

BRICK TOP
Pete, talk to me.

EXT. CAMPSITE – CONTINUOUS

Darren has a shotgun in one hand and Pete's mobile phone in the other.

> **DARREN**
> If you want your friend to hear ya, you'll have to talk a lot louder than that.

He looks away and shoots Pete.

EXT. WAREHOUSE – NIGHT

Brick Top hears the shot. We are back to Turkish, Tommy and Mickey emerging from the warehouse again and Brick Top tapping on the window of the car. Errol turns to look at the trio.

> **BRICK TOP**
> Give me that fuckin' shooter!

INT. BRICK TOP'S CAR OUTSIDE THE WAREHOUSE – NIGHT

This time we see that Mickey's men are in the car.

> **PATRICK**
> I'll give you your shooter, you cunt!

The window slides down. Brick Top stares down the barrels of two shotguns. He is shocked and Errol is looking the wrong way. Shots ring out.

EXT. WAREHOUSE – NIGHT – FLASHBACK

Flashback to Turkish, Tommy and Mickey looking towards us. The guns go off. Turkish and Tommy look petrified, Mickey is unmoved.

>   TURKISH (V/O)
> That is when I clocked the pikey had money riding on himself…

EXT. WAREHOUSE/BRICK TOP'S CAR

Mickey walks away from the other two towards Brick Top's car, stepping over Brick Top and Errol's bodies.

>   TURKISH (V/O cont'd)
> …That's the reason why the bastard never goes down when he's supposed to.

Mickey pauses by the car as Patrick and the other gypsy get out. A van pulls up to pick up Mickey and the boys.

>   TURKISH (V/O cont'd)
> We'd been tucked up…

EXT. WAREHOUSE/EXT. TOMMY'S CAR

Turkish is opening the door to his car. Tommy and he still look shocked.

>   TURKISH (V/O cont'd)
> …while he's been cleaning up.

EXT. WAREHOUSE/EXT. TOMMY'S CAR –
CONTINUOUS

The gypsy van pulls away.

> TURKISH (V/O cont'd)
> We're worse off now than when we started.

FADE TO BLACK.

EXT. DESERTED CAMPSITE

FADE UP FROM BLACK:

Turkish's V/O starts over black.

> TURKISH (V/O)
> The next day we went to the campsite. The gypsies had
> disappeared during the night…

Turkish and Tommy look around the deserted campsite.

> TURKISH (V/O)
> …which was probably a good thing. Considering they'd
> just buried twelve people somewhere in the area.

> TOMMY (off-camera)
> Where is he?

> TURKISH
> He ain't fuckin' here, that's for sure.

TOMMY

We can't ask a man to fight for us if we can't find him, can we?

TURKISH

You won't find a pikey that doesn't want to be found, Tommy. He could be in a campsite in Campofuckinchea by now. Ah bollocks! Come on.

They turn around to find heavy-looking characters by the Range Rover, checking it out. Two of the heavies walk over to Turkish and Tommy.

HEAVY

What you doing here?

TURKISH

What's it got to do with you?

The heavy proffers a police identity card. He's a copper. Pause. Turkish looks around. A dog arriving in the campsite. It's our friendly missing dog, last seen escaping from the pawnbrokers, pursued by Avi's shots.

TURKISH

Taking the dog for a walk. What's the problem?

COPPER

What's in the car?

TURKISH

Seats and a steering wheel.

CUT TO: a shot of the car boot. It's empty.

COPPER

What do you know about gypsies?

TURKISH

Know that they're not to be trusted.

HEAVY

All right, get your dog, on your way.

TURKISH

Get the dog, Tommy.

TOMMY

Eh?

TURKISH

The dog.

Tommy goes after the dog and tries to pick him up.

TOMMY

All right boy. Come on Daisy.

The dog runs off.

TOMMY (cont'd)

No, Daisy. Daisy!

Tommy gives chase.

TURKISH (to Copper)

He loves that dog.

Tommy is chasing the dog all over the campsite.

TURKISH (cont'd)
Always playing silly games. (To Tommy) Stop messing
about Tommy. Get it in the car. Tommy!

Tommy manages to catch the dog and pick him up.

TOMMY
Good boy. Good boy, Daisy.

'Daisy' squeaks as he's carried along.

INT. TURKISH'S CAR – DAY

Turkish drives along, the dog is on Tommy's lap squeaking.

EXT. COUNTRY LANE NR CAMPSITE – DAY –
CONTINUOUS

The police have stopped Sol and Vinny's car and they have
their hands on the roof as they are being frisked. Another
copper is opening the boot. Sol nudges Vinny as Turkish and
Tommy pass by slowly in their car – their eyes are caught by
the sight of the dog but there's nothing they can do now.

COPPER 2
Could you tell me why you have a dead man missing
an arm in your boot?

Sol shrugs.

COPPER 2
Hey George, is that a tea cosy on his head?

INT. TURKISH'S CAR – DAY– CONTINUOUS

Tommy strokes the dog.

> TURKISH
> Ohh you love a dog don't you, Tommy?

The car disappears down the road.

DISSOLVE TO REPEAT OF VERY FIRST SCENE/INTRO
CLOSE-UP BACK OF MAN'S HEAD.

We see Tommy and Turkish waiting in front of him again –
and also the dog is there wearing a surgical collar.

> TURKISH (V/O)
> Tommy persuaded me to keep the dog. I eventually agreed
> as long as he took it to a vet. I couldn't stand that
> squeaking anymore. The vet found half an undigested
> shoe, a squeaky toy and an 84 carat diamond lodged in its
> stomach. It's quite amazing what can happen in a week.

The dog barks.

> TURKISH (V/O cont'd)
> Still didn't shut it up though. So what do you do? You
> go to see the man that knows about these sort of things.

Turkish finally speaks.

> TURKISH
> So what do you think? Do you know anyone who'd be
> interested?

The camera spins round the desk to reveal the man's face –
it's Doug the Head.

                              DOUG
          I might.

He spins round, straight-faced, and picks up the phone.

And we go through the travel montage again:
CUT TO: Avi puts the phone down.
CUT TO: A NY taxi door slams.
CUT TO: Avi takes a pill on the plane.
CUT TO: Concorde takes off.
CUT TO: A hand comes down on a passport and stamps.

                          THE END